Natural Legal Language Processing Workshop (NLLP 2019)

Minneapolis, Minnesota, USA
7 June 2019

ISBN: 978-1-5108-8776-3

NAACL HLT 2019

Natural Legal Language Processing
(NLLP)

Proceedings of the 2019 Workshop

June 7, 2019
Minneapolis, MN

Introduction

Welcome to the first edition of the NLLP (Natural Legal Language Processing) Workshop, co-located with the 2019 Annual Conference of the North American Chapter of the Association for Computational Linguistics.

Many industries have embraced natural language processing (NLP) approaches, which have altered healthcare, finance, education and other fields. The legal domain however remains largely underrepresented in the NLP literature despite its enormous potential for generating interesting research problems. Electronic tools are increasingly used for all types of legal tasks and that use is predicted to grow sharply. By its very nature, the practice of law necessarily involves the analysis and interpretation of language. The potential for NLP applications to provide benefit to practitioners of law and consumers of legal services around the world is enormous.

We organized this workshop to bring together researchers and practitioners from around the world who develop NLP techniques for legal documents. This is an exciting opportunity to expand the boundaries of our field by identifying new problems and exploring new data as it interacts with the full inventory of NLP and machine learning approaches. In this spirit, the Organizing and Program Committee was assembled to include researchers from both academia and industry, from natural language processing and legal backgrounds.

We were interested in five types of papers: (1) applications of NLP methods to legal tasks; (2) experimental results using and adapting NLP methods in legal documents; (3) descriptions of new legal tasks for NLP; (4) creation of curated and/or annotated resources; (5) descriptions of systems which use NLP technologies for legal text. We also offered the option of submitting original unpublished research as non-archival in order to accommodate publication of the work at a later date in a conference or journal. These papers were reviewed following the same procedure as archival submissions.

We received 20 submissions and accepted 12 papers for an overall acceptance rate of 60 percent, all being presented orally. Out of the 12 accepted papers, 6 are long papers, 3 are short papers and 3 are original work submitted as non-archival. Half of the accepted papers have primarily industry authors. Each paper was reviewed by 3 to 5 members of the Program Committee. The papers cover a range of topics including bias in the judiciary, predictive methods for legal documents, building NLP tools to process legal documents and system descriptions for processing contracts or dockets.

We thank our two invited speakers for accepting our invitation. Both speakers are legal scholars with an interest in using artificial intelligence and natural language processing methods for legal analysis. We hope their talks offer a fresh perspective for the attendees. Prof. Arthur Dyevre presents a talk titled: 'Law as Data: The Promise and Challenges of Natural Language Processing for Legal Research' and Prof. Daniel M. Katz presents a talk titled: 'NLP & Law {Past, Present + Future}'.

We thank everyone who expressed interest in the workshop, all authors of submitted papers, members of the Program Committee who did an excellent job at reviewing papers given a short turnaround time, everyone attending the workshop, NAACL HLT 2019 for hosting us and the local, workshop and publication chairs for their support. We especially thank our sponsors – Bloomberg and Bloomberg Law – for their contributions.

We are looking forward to meeting the authors and the other participants in the workshop in Minneapolis.

The NLLP Workshop organizers.

http://nllpw.org

Organizers:

Nikolaos Aletras, University of Sheffield (UK)
Elliott Ash, ETH Zurich (Switzerland)
Leslie Barrett, Bloomberg Law (USA)
Daniel L. Chen, Toulouse School of Economics (France)
Adam Meyers, New York University (USA)
Daniel Preoţiuc-Pietro, Bloomberg LP (USA)
David Rosenberg, Bloomberg LP (USA)
Amanda Stent, Bloomberg LP (USA)

Program Committee:

Tomaso Agnoloni, Institute of Legal Information Theory and Technologies (Italy)
Ion Androutsopoulos, Athens University of Economics and Business (Greece)
Joan Bachenko, Linguistech LLC (USA)
Claire Cardie, Cornell University (USA)
Ilias Chalkidis, Athens University of Economics and Business (Greece)
Rajarathnam Chandramouli, Stevens Institute of Technology (USA)
Laura Chiticariu, IBM Research (USA)
Walter Daelemans, University of Antwerp (Belgium)
Marina Danilevsky, IBM Research (USA)
Stefania Degaetano-Ortlieb, Saarland University (Germany)
Luigi Di Caro, University of Turin (Italy)
Liviu P. Dinu, University of Bucharest (Romania)
Eileen Fitzpatrick, Montclair State University (USA)
Enrico Francesconi, Institute of Legal Information Theory and Technologies (Italy)
Frank S. Giaoui, Columbia Law School (USA)
Matthias Grabmair, Carnegie Mellon University (USA)
Ilan Kernerman, K Dictionaries (Israel)
Seth Kulick, University of Pennsylvania (USA)
Vasileios Lampos, University College London (UK)
Mark Liberman, University of Pennsylvania (USA)
Shervin Malmasi, Harvard Medical School (USA)
Elena Montiel, Universidad Politécnica de Madrid (Spain)
Paulo Quaresma, University of Évora (Portugal)
Georg Rehm, DFKI (Germany)
Victor Rodríguez-Doncel, Universidad Politécnica de Madrid (Spain)
Victoria Rubin, University of Western Ontario (Canada)
Eugene Santos, Thayer School of Engineering at Dartmouth (USA)
Maosong Sun, Tsinghua University (China)
Dimitrios Tsarapatsanis, University of York (UK)
Mihaela Vela, Saarland University (Germany)
Marc B. Vilain, MITRE Corp (USA)
Jianqian Wang, SUNY Buffalo (USA)
Adam Wyner, Swansea University (UK)
Diyi Yang, Georgia Institute of Technology (USA)
Marcos Zampieri, University of Wolverhampton (UK)

Invited Speakers:

Arthur Dyevre, Katholieke Universiteit Leuven (Belgium)
Daniel Martin Katz, Illinois Institute of Technology – Chicago Kent College of Law (USA)

Table of Contents

Conference Program

Friday, June 7, 2019

9:00–9:10   *Workshop Opening*

9:10–10:10   *Invited Speaker*

9:10–10:10   *Law as Data: The Promise and Challenges of Natural Language Processing for Legal Research*
Arthur Dyevre

10:10–10:30   *Bias*

10:10–10:30   *Implicit Bias in the Judiciary*
Daniel Chen, Elliott Ash and Arianna Ornaghi

10:30–11:00   *Coffee*

11:00–12:20   *NLP Applications*

11:00–11:20   *Plain English Summarization of Contracts*
Laura Manor and Junyi Jessy Li

11:20–11:40   *Question Answering for Privacy Policies: Combining Computational and Legal Perspectives*
Abhilasha Ravichander, Alan W Black, Thomas Norton, Shomir Wilson and Norman Sadeh

11:40–12:00   *Scalable Methods for Annotating Legal-Decision Corpora*
Lisa Ferro, John Aberdeen, Karl Branting, Craig Pfeifer, Alexander Yeh and Amartya Chakraborty

12:00–12:20   *The Extent of Repetition in Contract Language*
Dan Simonson, Daniel Broderick and Jonathan Herr

12:20–14:00   *Lunch*

Friday, June 7, 2019 (continued)

14:00–15:00 *Invited Speaker*

14:00–15:00 *NLP & Law {Past, Present + Future}*
Daniel Katz

15:00–15:30 *Short Papers*

15:00–15:15 *Sentence Boundary Detection in Legal Text*
George Sanchez

15:15–15:30 *Legal Linking: Citation Resolution and Suggestion in Constitutional Law*
Robert Shaffer and Stephen Mayhew

15:30–16:00 *Coffee*

16:00–17:00 *Demos*

16:00–16:20 *Litigation Analytics: Case Outcomes Extracted from US Federal Court Dockets*
Thomas Vacek, Ronald Teo, Dezhao Song, Timothy Nugent, Conner Cowling and
Frank Schilder

16:20–16:40 *Developing and Orchestrating a Portfolio of Natural Legal Language Processing
and Document Curation Services*
Georg Rehm, Julian Moreno-Schneider, Jorge Gracia, Artem Revenko, Victor
Mireles, Maria Khvalchik, Ilan Kernerman, Andis Lagzdins, Marcis Pinnis, Artus
Vasilevskis, Elena Leitner, Jan Milde and Pia Weißenhorn

16:40–17:00 *Transparent Linguistic Models for Contract Understanding and Comparison*
Arvind Agarwal, Laura Chiticariu, Poornima Chozhiyath Raman, Marina
Danilevsky, Diman Ghazi, Ankush Gupta, Shanmukh Guttula, Yannis Katsis,
Rajasekar Krishnamurthy, Yunyao Li, Shubham Mudgal, Vitobha Munigala,
Nicholas Phan, Dhaval Sonawane, Sneha Srinivasan, Sudarshan Thitte, Shivaku-
mar Vaithyanathan, Mitesh Vasa, Ramiya Venkatachalam, Vinitha Yaski and Huaiyu
Zhu

17:00–17:10 *Break*

17:10–17:50 *Prediction*

17:10–17:30 *Legal Area Classification: A Comparative Study of Text Classifiers on Singapore
Supreme Court Judgments*
Jerrold Soh, How Khang Lim and Ian Ernst Chai

Plain English Summarization of Contracts

Laura Manor
Department of Linguistics
The University of Texas at Austin
manor@utexas.edu

Junyi Jessy Li
Department of Linguistics
The University of Texas at Austin
jessy@austin.utexas.edu

Abstract

Unilateral contracts, such as terms of service, play a substantial role in modern digital life. However, few users read these documents before accepting the terms within, as they are too long and the language too complicated. We propose the task of summarizing such legal documents in plain English, which would enable users to have a better understanding of the terms they are accepting.

We propose an initial dataset of legal text snippets paired with summaries written in plain English. We verify the quality of these summaries manually and show that they involve heavy abstraction, compression, and simplification. Initial experiments show that unsupervised extractive summarization methods do not perform well on this task due to the level of abstraction and style differences. We conclude with a call for resource and technique development for simplification and style transfer for legal language.

1 Introduction

Although internet users accept unilateral contracts such as terms of service on a regular basis, it is well known that these users rarely read them. Nonetheless, these are binding contractual agreements. A recent study suggests that up to 98% of users do not fully read the terms of service before accepting them (Obar and Oeldorf-Hirsch, 2018). Additionally, they find that two of the top three factors users reported for not reading these documents were that they are perceived as too long ('information overload') and too complicated ('difficult to understand'). This can be seen in Table 1, where a section of the terms of service for a popular phone app includes a 78-word paragraph that can be distilled down to a 19-word summary.

The European Union's General Data Protection

Original Text: By using our Services, you are agreeing to these Terms, our Trainer Guidelines, and our Privacy Policy. If you are the parent or legal guardian of a child under the age of 13 (the Parent), you are agreeing to these Terms on behalf of yourself and your child(ren) who are authorized to use the Services pursuant to these Terms and in our Privacy Policy. If you dont agree to these Terms, our Trainer Guidelines, and our Privacy Policy, do not use the Services.

Human Summary: By playing this game, you agree to these terms. If you're under 13 and playing, your parent/guardian agrees on your behalf.

Table 1: Top: an excerpt from Niantic's Pokemon GO Terms of Service. Bottom: a summary written by a community member of TLDRLegal.

Regulation (2018)[1], the United States' Plain Writing Act (2010)[2], and New York State's Plain English law (1978) show that many levels of government have recognized the need to make legal information more accessible to non-legal communities. Additionally, due to recent social movements demanding accessible and transparent policies on the use of personal data on the internet (Sykuta et al., 2007), multiple online communities have formed that are dedicated to manually annotating various unilateral contracts.

We propose the task of the automatic summarization of legal documents *in plain English* for a non-legal audience. We hope that such a technological advancement would enable a greater number of people to enter into everyday contracts with a better understanding of what they are agreeing to. Automatic summarization is often used to reduce information overload, especially in the news domain (Nenkova et al., 2011). Summarization has been largely missing in the legal genre, with notable exceptions of judicial judgments (Farzindar and Lapalme, 2004; Hachey and Grover, 2006)

---

[1]https://eugdpr.org/
[2]https://plainlanguage.gov/

Proceedings of the Natural Legal Language Processing Workshop 2019, pages 1–11
Minneapolis, Minesotta, June 7, 2019. ©2019 Association for Computational Linguistics

and case reports (Galgani et al., 2012), as well as information extraction on patents (Tseng et al., 2007; Tang et al., 2012). While some companies have conducted proprietary research in the summarization of contracts, this information sits behind a large pay-wall and is geared toward law professionals rather than the general public.

In an attempt to motivate advancement in this area, we have collected 446 sets of contract sections and corresponding reference summaries which can be used as a test set for such a task.[3] We have compiled these sets from two websites dedicated to explaining complicated legal documents in plain English.

Rather than attempt to summarize an entire document, these sources summarize each document at the section level. In this way, the reader can reference the more detailed text if need be. The summaries in this dataset are reviewed for quality by the first author, who has 3 years of professional contract drafting experience.

The dataset we propose contains 446 sets of parallel text. We show the level of abstraction through the number of novel words in the reference summaries, which is significantly higher than the abstractive single-document summaries created for the shared tasks of the Document Understanding Conference (DUC) in 2002 (Over et al., 2007), a standard dataset used for single document news summarization. Additionally, we utilize several common readability metrics to show that there is an average of a 6 year reading level difference between the original documents and the reference summaries in our legal dataset.

In initial experimentation using this dataset, we employ popular unsupervised extractive summarization models such as TextRank (Mihalcea and Tarau, 2004) and Greedy KL (Haghighi and Vanderwende, 2009), as well as lead baselines. We show that such methods do not perform well on this dataset when compared to the same methods on DUC 2002. These results highlight the fact that this is a very challenging task. As there is not currently a dataset in this domain large enough for supervised methods, we suggest the use of methods developed for simplification and/or style transfer.

In this paper, we begin by discussing how this task relates to the current state of text summarization and similar tasks in Section 2. We then intro-

duce the novel dataset and provide details on the level of abstraction, compression, and readability in Section 3. Next, we provide results and analysis on the performance of extractive summarization baselines on our data in Section 5. Finally, we discuss the potential for unsupervised systems in this genre in Section 6.

2 Related work

Given a document, the goal of *single document summarization* is to produce a shortened summary of the document that captures its main semantic content (Nenkova et al., 2011). Existing research extends over several genres, including news (Over et al., 2007; See et al., 2017; Grusky et al., 2018), scientific writing (TAC, 2014; Jaidka et al., 2016; Yasunaga et al., 2019), legal case reports (Galgani et al., 2012), etc. A critical factor in successful summarization research is the availability of a dataset with parallel document/human-summary pairs for system evaluation. However, no such publicly available resource for summarization of contracts exists to date. We present the first dataset in this genre. Note that unlike other genres where human summaries paired with original documents can be found at scale, e.g., the CNN/DailyMail dataset (See et al., 2017), resources of this kind are yet to be curated/created for contracts. As traditional supervised summarization systems require these types of large datasets, the resources released here are intended for evaluation, rather than training. Additionally, as a first step, we restrict our initial experiments to unsupervised baselines which do not require training on large datasets.

The dataset we present summarizes contracts in *plain English*. While there is no precise definition of plain English, the general philosophy is to make a text readily accessible for as many English speakers as possible. (Mellinkoff, 2004; Tiersma, 2000). Guidelines for plain English often suggest a preference for words with Saxon etymologies rather than a Latin/Romance etymologies, the use of short words, sentences, and paragraphs, etc.[4] (Tiersma, 2000; Kimble, 2006). In this respect, the proposed task involves some level of *text simplification*, as we will discuss in Section 4.2. However, existing resources for text simplification target literacy/reading levels (Xu et al., 2015) or learners of English as a second language (Zhu et al., 2010). Additionally, these models are trained us-

---

[3]The dataset is available at `https://github.com/lauramanor/legal_summarization`

[4]`https://plainlanguage.gov/guidelines/`

ing Wikipedia or news articles, which are quite different from legal documents. These systems are trained without access to sentence-aligned parallel corpora; they only require semantically similar texts (Shen et al., 2017; Yang et al., 2018; Li et al., 2018). To the best of our knowledge, however, there is no existing dataset to facilitate the transfer of legal language to plain English.

3 Data

This section introduces a dataset compiled from two websites dedicated to explaining unilateral contracts in plain English: TL;DRLegal[5] and TOS;DR[6]. These websites clarify language within legal documents by providing summaries for specific sections of the original documents. The data was collected using Scrapy[7] and a JSON interface provided by each website's API. Summaries are submitted and maintained by members of the website community; neither website requires community members to be law professionals.

3.1 TL;DRLegal

TL;DRLegal focuses mostly on software licenses, however, we only scraped documents related to specific companies rather than generic licenses (i.e. Creative Commons, etc). The scraped data consists of 84 sets sourced from 9 documents: Pokemon GO Terms of Service, TLDRLegal Terms of Service, Minecraft End User Licence Agreement, YouTube Terms of Service, Android SDK License Agreement (June 2014), Google Play Game Services (May 15th, 2013), Facebook Terms of Service (Statement of Rights and Responsibilities), Dropbox Terms of Service, and Apple Website Terms of Service.

Each set consists of a portion from the original agreement text and a summary written in plain English. Examples of the original text and the summary are shown in Table 2.

3.2 TOS;DR

TOS;DR tends to focus on topics related to user data and privacy. We scraped 421 sets of parallel text sourced from 166 documents by 122 companies. Each set consists of a portion of an agreement text (e.g., Terms of Use, Privacy Policy, Terms of Service) and 1-3 human-written summaries.

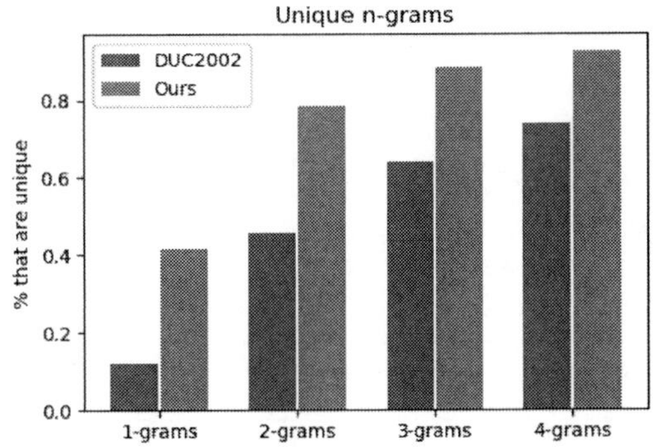

Figure 1: Unique n-grams in the reference summary, contrasting our legal dataset with DUC 2002 single document summarization data.

While the multiple references can be useful for system development and evaluation, the qualities of these summaries varied greatly. Therefore, each text was examined by the first author, who has three years of professional experience in contract drafting for a software company. A total of 361 sets had at least one quality summary in the set. For each, the annotator selected the most informative summary to be used in this paper.

Of the 361 accepted summaries, more than two-thirds of them (152) are 'templatic' summaries. A summary deemed templatic if it could be found in more than one summary set, either word-for-word or with just the service name changed. However, of the 152 templatic summaries which were selected as the best of their set, there were 111 unique summaries. This indicates that the templatic summaries which were selected for the final dataset are relatively unique.

A total of 369 summaries were outright rejected for a variety of reasons, including summaries that: were a repetition of another summary for the same source snippet (291), were an exact quote of the original text (63), included opinionated language that could not be inferred from the original text (24), or only described the topic of the quote but not the content (20). We also rejected any summaries that are longer than the original texts they summarize. Annotated examples from TOS;DR can be found in Table 3.

4 Analysis

4.1 Levels of abstraction and compression

To understand the level of abstraction of the proposed dataset, we first calculate the number of n-

Source	Facebook Terms of Service (Statement of Rights and Responsibilities) - November 15, 2013
Original Text	Our goal is to deliver advertising and other commercial or sponsored content that is valuable to our users and advertisers. In order to help us do that, you agree to the following: You give us permission to use your name, profile picture, content, and information in connection with commercial, sponsored, or related content (such as a brand you like) served or enhanced by us. This means, for example, that you permit a business or other entity to pay us to display your name and/or profile picture with your content or information, without any compensation to you. If you have selected a specific audience for your content or information, we will respect your choice when we use it. We do not give your content or information to advertisers without your consent. You understand that we may not always identify paid services and communications as such.
Summary	Facebook can use any of your stuff for any reason they want without paying you, for advertising in particular.
Source	Pokemon GO Terms of Service - July 1, 2016
Original Text	We may cancel, suspend, or terminate your Account and your access to your Trading Items, Virtual Money, Virtual Goods, the Content, or the Services, in our sole discretion and without prior notice, including if (a) your Account is inactive (i.e., not used or logged into) for one year; (b) you fail to comply with these Terms; (c) we suspect fraud or misuse by you of Trading Items, Virtual Money, Virtual Goods, or other Content; (d) we suspect any other unlawful activity associated with your Account; or (e) we are acting to protect the Services, our systems, the App, any of our users, or the reputation of Niantic, TPC, or TPCI. We have no obligation or responsibility to, and will not reimburse or refund, you for any Trading Items, Virtual Money, or Virtual Goods lost due to such cancellation, suspension, or termination. You acknowledge that Niantic is not required to provide a refund for any reason, and that you will not receive money or other compensation for unused Virtual Money and Virtual Goods when your Account is closed, whether such closure was voluntary or involuntary. We have the right to offer, modify, eliminate, and/or terminate Trading Items, Virtual Money, Virtual Goods, the Content, and/or the Services, or any portion thereof, at any time, without notice or liability to you. If we discontinue the use of Virtual Money or Virtual Goods, we will provide at least 60 days advance notice to you by posting a notice on the Site or App or through other communications.
Summary	If you haven't played for a year, you mess up, or we mess up, we can delete all of your virtual goods. We don't have to give them back. We might even discontinue some virtual goods entirely, but we'll give you 60 days advance notice if that happens.
Source	Apple Website Terms of Service - Nov. 20, 2009
Original Text	Any feedback you provide at this site shall be deemed to be non-confidential. Apple shall be free to use such information on an unrestricted basis.
Summary	Apple may use your feedback without restrictions (e.g. share it publicly.)

Table 2: Examples of summary sets from TLDRLegal.

Original Text	When you upload, submit, store, send or receive content to or through our Services, you give Google (and those we work with) a worldwide license to use, host, store, reproduce, modify, create derivative works (such as those resulting from translations, adaptations or other changes we make so that your content works better with our Services), communicate, publish, publicly perform, publicly display and distribute such content.
Summary1 (best)	The copyright license you grant is for the limited purpose of operating, promoting, and improving existing and new Google Services. However, please note that the license does not end if you stop using the Google services.
Summary2	The copyright license that users grant this service is limited to the parties that make up the service's broader platform.
Summary3	Limited copyright license to operate and improve all Google Services
Original Text	We may share information with vendors, consultants, and other service providers (but not with advertisers and ad partners) who need access to such information to carry out work for us. The partners use of personal data will be subject to appropriate confidentiality and security measures.
Summary1 (best)	Reddit shares data with third parties
Summary2	Third parties may be involved in operating the service
Summary3 (rejected)	Third parties may be involved in operating the service

Table 3: Examples from TOS;DR. Contract sections from TOS;DR included up to three summaries. In each case, the summaries were inspected for quality. Only the best summary was included in the analysis in this paper.

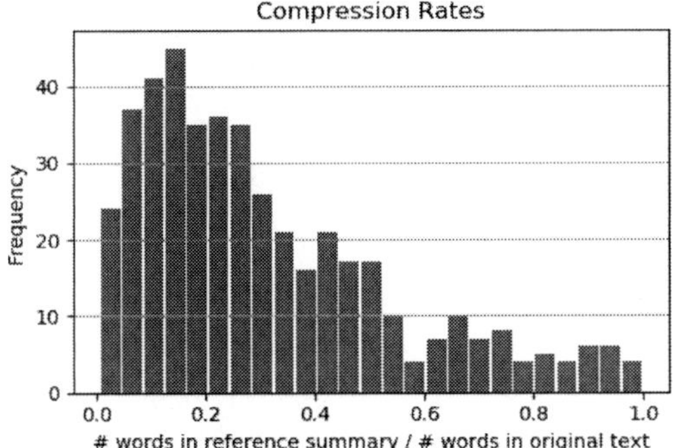

Figure 2: Ratio of words in the reference summary to words in the original text. The ratio was calculated by dividing the number of words in the reference summary by the number of words in the original text.

grams that appear only in the reference summaries and not in the original texts they summarize (See et al., 2017; Chen and Bansal, 2018). As shown in Figure 1, 41.4% of words in the reference summaries did not appear in the original text. Additionally, 78.5%, 88.4%, and 92.3% of 2-, 3-, and 4-grams in the reference summaries did not appear in the original text. When compared to a standard abstractive news dataset also shown in the graph (DUC 2002), the legal dataset is significantly more abstractive.

Furthermore, as shown in Figure 2, the dataset is very compressive, with a mean compression rate of 0.31 (std 0.23). The original texts have a mean of 3.6 (std 3.8) sentences per document and a mean of 105.6 (std 147.8) words per document. The reference summaries have a mean of 1.2 (std 0.6) sentences per document, and a mean of 17.2 (std 11.8) words per document.

4.2 Readability

To verify that the summaries more accessible to a wider audience, we also compare the readability of the reference summaries and the original texts.

Full texts We make a comparison between the original contract sections and respective summaries using four common readability metrics. All readability metrics were implemented using Wim Muskee's readability calculator library for Python[8]. These measurements included:

- **Flesch-Kincaid formula (F-K)**: the weighted sum of the number of words

[8] https://github.com/wimmuskee/readability-score

	F-K	C-L	SMOG	ARI	Avg
Ref	12.66	15.11	14.14	12.98	13.29
Orig	20.22	16.53	19.58	22.24	19.29

Table 4: Average readability scores for the reference summaries (Ref) and the original texts (Orig). Descriptions of each measurement can be found in Section 4.2.

in a sentence and the number of syllables per word (Kincaid et al., 1975),

- **Coleman-Liau index (CL)**: the weighted sum of the number of letters per 100 words and the average number of sentences per 100 words (Coleman and Liau, 1975),

- **SMOG**: the weighted square root of the number of polysyllable words per sentence (Mc Laughlin, 1969), and

- **Automated readability index** (ARI): the weighted sum of the number of characters per word and number of words per sentence (Senter and Smith, 1967).

Though these metrics were originally formulated based on US grade levels, we have adjusted the numbers to provide the equivalent age correlated with the respective US grade level.

We ran each measurement on the reference summaries and original texts. As shown in Table 4, the reference summaries scored lower than the original texts for each test by an average of 6 years.

Words We also seek to single out lexical difficulty, as legal text often contains vocabulary that is difficult for non-professionals. To do this, we obtain the top 50 words W_s most associated with summaries and top 50 words W_d most associated with the original snippets (described below) and consider the *differences* of ARI and F-K measures. We chose these two measures because they are a weighted sum of a word and sentential properties; as sentential information is kept the same (50 1-word "sentences"), the *differences* will reflect the change in readability of the words most associated with plain English summaries/original texts.

To collect W_s and W_d, we calculate the log odds ratio for each word, a measure used in prior work comparing summary text and original documents (Nye and Nenkova, 2015). The log odds ratio compares the probability of a word w occurring in the set of all summaries S vs. original texts D:

Original Text: arise, unless, receive, whether, example, signal, b, technology, identifier, expressly, transmit, visit, perform, search, partner, understand, conduct, server, child, support, regulation, base, similar, purchase, automatically, mobile, agent, derivative, either, commercial, reasonable, cause, functionality, advertiser, act, ii, thereof, arbitrator, attorney, modification, locate, c, individual, form, following, accordance, hereby, cookie, apps, advertisement

Reference Summary: fingerprint, fit, header, targeted, involve, pixel, advance, quality, track, want, stuff, even, guarantee, maintain, beacon, ban, month, prohibit, allow, defend, notification, ownership, acceptance, delete, user, prior, reason, hold, notify, govern, keep, class, change, might, illegal, old, harmless, indemnify, see, assume, deletion, waive, stop, operate, year, enforce, target, many, constitute, posting

Table 5: The 50 words most associated with the original text or reference summary, as measured by the log odds ratio.

$$log\left(\frac{Odds(w, S)}{Odds(w, D)}\right) \simeq log\left(\frac{P(w|S)}{P(w|D)}\right)$$

The list of words with the highest log odds ratios for the reference summaries (W_s) and original texts (W_d) can be found in Table 5.

We calculate the differences (in years) of ARI and F-K scores between W_s and W_d:

$$ARI(W_d) - ARI(W_s) = 5.66$$

$$FK(W_d) - FK(W_s) = 6.12$$

Hence, there is a ~6-year reading level distinction between the two sets of words, an indication that lexical difficulty is paramount in legal text.

5 Summarization baselines

We present our legal dataset as a test set for contracts summarization. In this section, we report baseline performances of *unsupervised, extractive* methods as most recent supervised abstractive summarization methods, e.g., Rush et al. (2015), See et al. (2017), would not have enough training data in this domain. We chose to look at the following common baselines:

- **TextRank** Proposed by Mihalcea and Tarau (2004), TextRank harnesses the PageRank algorithm to choose the sentences with the highest similarity scores to the original document.[9]

- **KLSum** An algorithm introduced by (Haghighi and Vanderwende, 2009) which greedily selects the sentences that minimize the Kullback-Lieber (KL) divergence between the original text and proposed summary.

- **Lead-1** A common baseline in news summarization is to select the first 1-3 sentences of the original text as the summary (See et al., 2017). With this dataset, we include the first sentence as the summary as it is the closest to the average number of sentences per reference (1.2).

- **Lead-K** A variation of Lead-1, this baseline selects the first k sentences until a word limit is satisfied.

- **Random-K** This baseline selects a random sentence until a word limit is satisfied. For this baseline, the reported numbers are an average of 10 runs on the entire dataset.

Settings We employ lowercasing and lemmatization, as well as remove stop words and punctuation during pre-processing[10]. For TextRank, KLSum, Lead-K, and Random-K, we produce summaries budgeted at the average number of words among all summaries (Rush et al., 2015). However, for the sentence which causes the summary to exceed the budget, we keep or discard the full sentence depending on which resulting summary is closer to the budgeted length.

Results To gain a quantitative understanding of the baseline results, we employed ROUGE (Lin, 2004). ROUGE is a standard metric used for evaluating summaries based on the lexical overlap between a generated summary and gold/reference summaries. The ROUGE scores for the unsupervised summarization baselines found in this paper can be found in Table 6.

In the same table, we also tabulate ROUGE scores of the same baselines run on DUC 2002 (Over et al., 2007), 894 documents with summary lengths of 100 words, following the same settings. Note that our performance is a bit different from reported numbers in Mihalcea and Tarau (2004), as we performed different pre-processing and the summary lengths were not processed in the same way.

---

[9]For this paper we utilized the TextRank package from Summa NLP: https://github.com/summanlp/textrank

[10]NLTK was used for lemmatization and identification of stop words.

	TLDRLegal			TOS;DR			Combined			DUC 2002		
	R-1	R-2	R-L	R-1	R-2	R-L	R-1	R-2	R-L	R-1	R-2	R-L
TextRank	**25.60**	8.05	**18.62**	23.88	6.96	16.96	24.03	7.16	17.10	40.94	18.89	36.70
KLSum	24.98	7.84	18.08	23.25	6.76	16.67	23.56	6.94	16.93	40.06	16.94	35.85
Lead-1	23.09	**8.23**	17.10	24.05	7.30	17.22	23.87	7.47	17.19	29.66	13.76	19.46
Lead-K	24.04	8.14	17.46	**24.47**	**7.40**	**17.66**	**24.38**	**7.52**	**17.63**	**43.57**	**21.69**	**39.49**
Random-K	21.94	6.19	15.84	22.39	6.17	16.01	22.32	6.33	16.09	35.75	14.12	31.91

Table 6: Performance for each dataset on the baselines was measured using Rouge-1, Rouge-2, and Rouge-L.

Crucially, ROUGE scores are much higher on DUC 2002 than on our legal dataset. We speculate that this is due to the highly abstractive nature of this data, in addition to the divergent styles of the summaries and original texts.

In general, Lead-K performed best on both TOS;DR and DUC 2002. The performance gap between TextRank and Lead-K is much larger on DUC 2002 than on our dataset. On the legal datasets, TextRank outperformed Lead-K on TL-DRLegal and is very close to the performance of Lead-K on TOS;DR. Additionally, Random-K performed only about 2 ROUGE points lower than Lead-K on our dataset, while it scored almost 8 points lower on the DUC 2002 dataset. We attribute this to the structure of the original text; news articles (i.e. DUC 2002) follow the inverse pyramid structure where the first few sentences give an overview of the story, and the rest of the article content is diverse. In contracts, the sentences in each section are more similar to each other lexically.

Qualitative Analysis We examined some of the results of the unsupervised extractive techniques to get a better understanding of what methods might improve the results. Select examples can be found in Table 7.

As shown by example (1), the extractive systems performed well when the reference summaries were either an extract or a compressed version of the original text. However, examples (2-4) show various ways the extractive systems were not able to perform well.

In (2), the extractive systems were able to select an appropriate sentence, but the sentence is much more complex than the reference summary. Utilizing text simplification techniques may help in these circumstances.

In (3), we see that the reference summary is much better able to abstract over a larger portion of the original text than the selected sentences. (3a)

shows that by having much shorter sentences, the reference summary is able to cover more of the original text. (3b) is able to restate 651-word original text in 11 words.

Finally, in (4), the sentences from the original text are extremely long, and thus the automated summaries, while only having one sentence, are 711 and 136 words respectively. Here, we also see that the reference summaries have a much different style than the original text.

6 Discussion

Our preliminary experiments and analysis show that summarizing legal contracts in plain English is challenging, and point to the potential usefulness of a simplification or style transfer system in the summarization pipeline. Yet this is challenging. First, there may be a substantial domain gap between legal documents and texts that existing simplification systems are trained on (e.g., Wikipedia, news). Second, popular supervised approaches such as treating sentence simplification as monolingual machine translation (Specia, 2010; Zhu et al., 2010; Woodsend and Lapata, 2011; Xu et al., 2016; Zhang and Lapata, 2017) would be difficult to apply due to the lack of sentence-aligned parallel corpora. Possible directions include unsupervised lexical simplification utilizing distributed representations of words (Glavaš and Štajner, 2015; Paetzold and Specia, 2016), unsupervised sentence simplification using rich semantic structure (Narayan and Gardent, 2016), or unsupervised style transfer techniques (Shen et al., 2017; Yang et al., 2018; Li et al., 2018). However, there is not currently a dataset in this domain large enough for unsupervised methods, nor corpora unaligned but comparable in semantics across legal and plain English, which we see as a call for future research.

(1a)	Reference Summary	librarything will not sell or give personally identifiable information to any third party.
	Textrank, Lead-K	no sale of personal information. librarything will not sell or give personally identifiable information to any third party.
	KLSum	this would be evil and we are not evil.
(1b)	Reference Summary	you are responsible for maintaining the security of your account and for the activities on your account
	TextRank, KLSum, Lead-K	you are responsible for maintaining the confidentiality of your password and account if any and are fully responsible for any and all activities that occur under your password or account
(2a)	Reference Summary	if you offer suggestions to the service they become the owner of the ideas that you give them
	TextRank, KLSum, Lead-K	if you provide a submission whether by email or otherwise you agree that it is non confidential unless couchsurfing states otherwise in writing and shall become the sole property of couchsurfing
(2b)	Reference Summary	when the service wants to change its terms users are notified a month or more in advance.
	TextRank	in this case you will be notified by e mail of any amendment to this agreement made by valve within 60 sixty days before the entry into force of the said amendment.
(2c)	Reference Summary	you cannot delete your account for this service.
	TextRank, KLSum, Lead-K	please note that we have no obligation to delete any of stories favorites or comments listed in your profile or otherwise remove their association with your profile or username.
(3a)	Original Text	by using our services you are agreeing to these terms our trainer guidelines and our privacy policy. if you are the parent or legal guardian of a child under the age of 13 the parent you are agreeing to these terms on behalf of yourself and your child ren who are authorized to use the services pursuant to these terms and in our privacy policy. if you don t agree to these terms our trainer guidelines and our privacy policy do not use the services.
	Reference Summary	if you don t agree to these terms our trainer guidelines and our privacy policy do not use the services.
	TextRank	by playing this game you agree to these terms. if you re under 13 and playing your parent guardian agrees on your behalf.
	KLSum, Lead-K	by using our services you are agreeing to these terms our trainer guidelines and our privacy policy.
(3b)	Original Text	subject to your compliance with these terms niantic grants you a limited nonexclusive nontransferable non sublicensable license to download and install a copy of the app on a mobile device and to run such copy of the app solely for your own personal noncommercial purposes. [...] by using the app you represent and warrant that i you are not located in a country that is subject to a u s government embargo or that has been designated by the u s government as a terrorist supporting country and ii you are not listed on any u s government list of prohibited or restricted parties.
	Reference Summary	don t copy modify resell distribute or reverse engineer this app.
	TextRank	in the event of any third party claim that the app or your possession and use of the app infringes that third party s intellectual property rights niantic will be solely responsible for the investigation defense settlement and discharge of any such intellectual property infringement claim to the extent required by these terms.
	KLSum	if you accessed or downloaded the app from any app store or distribution platform like the apple store google play or amazon appstore each an app provider then you acknowledge and agree that these terms are concluded between you and niantic and not with app provider and that as between us and the app provider niantic is solely responsible for the app.
(4a)	Reference Summary	don t be a jerk. don t hack or cheat. we don t have to ban you but we can. we ll also cooperate with law enforcement.
	KLSum	by way of example and not as a limitation you agree that when using the services and content you will not defame abuse harass harm stalk threaten or otherwise violate the legal rights including the rights of privacy and publicity of others [...] lease the app or your account collect or store any personally identifiable information from the services from other users of the services without their express permission violate any applicable law or regulation or enable any other individual to do any of the foregoing.
(4b)	Reference Summary	don t blame google.
	TextRank, KLSum, Lead-K	the indemnification provision in section 9 of the api tos is deleted in its entirety and replaced with the following you agree to hold harmless and indemnify google and its subsidiaries affiliates officers agents and employees or partners from and against any third party claim arising from or in any way related to your misuse of google play game services your violation of these terms or any third party s misuse of google play game services or actions that would constitute a violation of these terms provided that you enabled such third party to access the apis or failed to take reasonable steps to prevent such third party from accessing the apis including any liability or expense arising from all claims losses damages actual and consequential suits judgments litigation costs and attorneys fees of every kind and nature.

Table 7: Examples of reference summaries and results from various extractive summarization techniques. The text shown here has been pre-processed. To conserve space, original texts were excluded from most examples.

7 Conclusion

In this paper, we propose the task of summarizing legal documents in plain English and present an initial evaluation dataset for this task. We gather our dataset from online sources dedicated to explaining sections of contracts in plain English and manually verify the quality of the summaries. We show that our dataset is highly abstractive and that the summaries are much simpler to read. This task is challenging, as popular unsupervised extractive summarization methods do not perform well on this dataset and, as discussed in section 6, current methods that address the change in register are mostly supervised as well. We call for the development of resources for unsupervised simplification and style transfer in this domain.

Acknowledgments

We would like to personally thank Katrin Erk for her help in the conceptualization of this project. Additional thanks to May Helena Plumb, Barea Sinno, and David Beavers for their aid in the revision process. We are grateful for the anonymous reviewers and for the TLDRLegal and TOS;DR communities and their pursuit of transparency.

References

Yen-Chun Chen and Mohit Bansal. 2018. Fast abstractive summarization with reinforce-selected sentence rewriting. In *Proceedings of the 56th Annual Meeting of the Association for Computational Linguistics (Vol 1: Long Papers)*, pages 675–686.

Meri Coleman and Ta Lin Liau. 1975. A computer readability formula designed for machine scoring. *Journal of Applied Psychology*, 60(2):283.

Atefeh Farzindar and Guy Lapalme. 2004. Legal text summarization by exploration of the thematic structure and argumentative roles. *Text Summarization Branches Out*.

Filippo Galgani, Paul Compton, and Achim Hoffmann. 2012. Combining different summarization techniques for legal text. In *Proceedings of the Workshop on Innovative Hybrid Approaches to the Processing of Textual Data*, pages 115–123.

General Data Protection Regulation. 2018. Regulation on the protection of natural persons with regard to the processing of personal data and on the free movement of such data, and repealing directive 95/46/ec (data protection directive). L119, 4 May 2016, pages 188.

Goran Glavaš and Sanja Štajner. 2015. Simplifying lexical simplification: Do we need simplified corpora? In *Proceedings of the 53rd Annual Meeting of the Association for Computational Linguistics and the 7th International Joint Conference on Natural Language Processing (Vol 2: Short Papers)*, pages 63–68.

Max Grusky, Mor Naaman, and Yoav Artzi. 2018. Newsroom: A dataset of 1.3 million summaries with diverse extractive strategies. In *Proceedings of the 2018 Conference of the North American Chapter of the Association for Computational Linguistics: Human Language Technologies, Volume 1 (Long Papers)*, pages 708–719.

Ben Hachey and Claire Grover. 2006. Extractive summarisation of legal texts. *Artificial Intelligence and Law*, 14(4):305–345.

Aria Haghighi and Lucy Vanderwende. 2009. Exploring content models for multi-document summarization. In *Proceedings of Human Language Technologies: The 2009 Annual Conference of the North American Chapter of the Association for Computational Linguistics*, pages 362–370.

Kokil Jaidka, Muthu Kumar Chandrasekaran, Sajal Rustagi, and Min-Yen Kan. 2016. Overview of the cl-scisumm 2016 shared task. In *Proceedings of the Joint Workshop on Bibliometric-enhanced Information Retrieval and Natural Language Processing for Digital Libraries*, pages 93–102.

Joseph Kimble. 2006. *Lifting the fog of legalese: essays on plain language*. Carolina Academic Press.

J Peter Kincaid, Robert P Fishburne Jr, Richard L Rogers, and Brad S Chissom. 1975. Derivation of new readability formulas (automated readability index, fog count and flesch reading ease formula) for navy enlisted personnel. In *Technical Report, Institute for Simulation and Training, University of Central Florida*.

Juncen Li, Robin Jia, He He, and Percy Liang. 2018. Delete, retrieve, generate: a simple approach to sentiment and style transfer. In *Proceedings of the 2018 Conference of the North American Chapter of the Association for Computational Linguistics: Human Language Technologies, Volume 1 (Long Papers)*, pages 1865–1874.

Chin-Yew Lin. 2004. ROUGE: A package for automatic evaluation of summaries. In *Text Summarization Branches Out*.

G Harry Mc Laughlin. 1969. Smog grading-a new readability formula. *Journal of reading*, 12(8):639–646.

David Mellinkoff. 2004. *The language of the law*. Wipf and Stock Publishers.

Rada Mihalcea and Paul Tarau. 2004. Textrank: Bringing order into text. In *Proceedings of the 2004 conference on empirical methods in natural language processing*.

Shashi Narayan and Claire Gardent. 2016. Unsupervised sentence simplification using deep semantics. In *The 9th International Natural Language Generation conference*, pages 111–120.

Ani Nenkova, Kathleen McKeown, et al. 2011. Automatic summarization. *Foundations and Trends® in Information Retrieval*, 5(2–3):103–233.

Benjamin Nye and Ani Nenkova. 2015. Identification and characterization of newsworthy verbs in world news. In *Proceedings of the 2015 Conference of the North American Chapter of the Association for Computational Linguistics: Human Language Technologies*, pages 1440–1445.

Jonathan A Obar and Anne Oeldorf-Hirsch. 2018. The biggest lie on the internet: Ignoring the privacy policies and terms of service policies of social networking services. *Information, Communication & Society*, pages 1–20.

Paul Over, Hoa Dang, and Donna Harman. 2007. DUC in context. *Information Processing & Management*, 43(6):1506–1520.

Gustavo H. Paetzold and Lucia Specia. 2016. Unsupervised lexical simplification for non-native speakers. In *Proceedings of the 13th Association for the Advancement of Artificial Intelligence Conference on Artificial Intelligence*, pages 3761–3767.

Plain English law. 1978. Title 7: Requirements for use of plain language in consumer transactions. The Laws Of New York Consolidated Laws. General Obligations. Article 5: Creation, Definition And Enforcement Of Contractual Obligations.

Plain Writing Act. 2010. An act to enhance citizen access to government information and services by establishing that government documents issued to the public must be written clearly, and for other purposes. House of Representatives 946; Public Law No. 111-274; 124 Statues at Large 2861.

Alexander M. Rush, Sumit Chopra, and Jason Weston. 2015. A neural attention model for abstractive sentence summarization. In *Proceedings of the 2015 Conference on Empirical Methods in Natural Language Processing*, pages 379–389.

Abigail See, Peter J Liu, and Christopher D Manning. 2017. Get to the point: Summarization with pointer-generator networks. In *Proceedings of the 55th Annual Meeting of the Association for Computational Linguistics (Vol 1: Long Papers)*, pages 1073–1083.

RJ Senter and Edgar A Smith. 1967. Automated readability index. Technical report, Cincinnati Univ OH.

Tianxiao Shen, Tao Lei, Regina Barzilay, and Tommi Jaakkola. 2017. Style transfer from non-parallel text by cross-alignment. In *Advances in neural information processing systems*, pages 6830–6841.

Lucia Specia. 2010. Translating from complex to simplified sentences. In *Proceedings of the International Conference on Computational Processing of the Portuguese Language*, pages 30–39.

Michael E Sykuta, Peter G Klein, and James Cutts. 2007. Cori k-base: Data overview.

TAC. 2014. In *https://tac.nist.gov/2014/BiomedSumm/*.

Jie Tang, Bo Wang, Yang Yang, Po Hu, Yanting Zhao, Xinyu Yan, Bo Gao, Minlie Huang, Peng Xu, Weichang Li, et al. 2012. Patentminer: topic-driven patent analysis and mining. In *Proceedings of the 18th Internationasl Conference on Knowledge Discovery and Data Mining*, pages 1366–1374.

Peter M Tiersma. 2000. *Legal language*. University of Chicago Press.

Yuen-Hsien Tseng, Chi-Jen Lin, and Yu-I Lin. 2007. Text mining techniques for patent analysis. *Information Processing & Management*, 43(5):1216–1247.

Kristian Woodsend and Mirella Lapata. 2011. Learning to simplify sentences with quasi-synchronous grammar and integer programming. In *Proceedings of the conference on empirical methods in natural language processing*, pages 409–420.

Wei Xu, Chris Callison-Burch, and Courtney Napoles. 2015. Problems in current text simplification research: New data can help. *Transactions of the Association for Computational Linguistics*, 3:283–297.

Wei Xu, Courtney Napoles, Ellie Pavlick, Quanze Chen, and Chris Callison-Burch. 2016. Optimizing statistical machine translation for text simplification. *Transactions of the Association for Computational Linguistics*, 4:401–415.

Zichao Yang, Zhiting Hu, Chris Dyer, Eric P Xing, and Taylor Berg-Kirkpatrick. 2018. Unsupervised text style transfer using language models as discriminators. In *Advances in Neural Information Processing Systems*, pages 7298–7309.

Michihiro Yasunaga, Jungo Kasai, Rui Zhang, Alexander R Fabbri Irene Li Dan, and Friedman Dragomir R Radev. 2019. Scisummnet: A large annotated corpus and content-impact models for scientific paper summarization with citation networks. In *Proceedings of the 13th Association for the Advancement of Artificial Intelligence Conference on Artificial Intelligence*.

Xingxing Zhang and Mirella Lapata. 2017. Sentence simplification with deep reinforcement learning. In *Proceedings of the 2017 Conference on Empirical Methods in Natural Language Processing*, pages 584–594.

Zhemin Zhu, Delphine Bernhard, and Iryna Gurevych.
2010. A monolingual tree-based translation model
for sentence simplification. In *Proceedings of the
23rd international conference on computational linguistics*, pages 1353–1361.

Scalable Methods for Annotating Legal-Decision Corpora

Lisa Ferro, John Aberdeen, Karl Branting, Craig Pfeifer,
Alexander Yeh, Amartya Chakraborty
The MITRE Corporation
{lferro, aberdeen, lbranting, cpfeifer, asy, achakraborty}@mitre.org

Abstract

Recent research has demonstrated that judicial and administrative decisions can be predicted by machine-learning models trained on prior decisions. However, to have any practical application, these predictions must be explainable, which in turn requires modeling a rich set of features. Such approaches face a roadblock if the knowledge engineering required to create these features is not scalable. We present an approach to developing a feature-rich corpus of administrative rulings about domain name disputes, an approach which leverages a small amount of manual annotation and prototypical patterns present in the case documents to automatically extend feature labels to the entire corpus. To demonstrate the feasibility of this approach, we report results from systems trained on this dataset.

1 Introduction

Recent research has demonstrated that judicial and administrative decisions can be predicted by machine-learning models trained on prior decisions (Medvedeva et al., 2018). Predictive legal models have the potential to improve both the delivery of services to citizens and the efficiency of agency decision processes, e.g., by making benefits adjudications faster and more transparent, and by enabling decision-support tools for evaluating benefits claims.

The accuracy of predictive legal models is highest, and explanatory capability greatest, when the prior decisions are represented in terms of features manually engineered to express exactly the most relevant aspects of the prior case (Katz et al., 2017). However, this approach is not scalable. Alternatively, decisions can be predicted from case text alone, but these models typically lack explanatory capability (Aletras et al., 2016). Development of approaches for explaining decision predictions in terms of relevant case facts while minimizing manual feature engineering is critical for broad adoption of systems for legal case prediction.

Our approach to explainable legal prediction focuses on annotating the portions of written decisions that set forth the justification for the decision. We hypothesize that tag sets for these justifications can be used as features for explainable prediction. In a separate paper (Branting et al., 2019) we propose an approach that uses models trained on an annotated corpus to extract features that can be used for both outcome prediction and explanation in new cases. This paper focuses on development of the annotated corpus itself.

Our feature set makes use of two common elements in legal argumentation: *issues* and *factors*. In our usage, an "issue" is a formal element of a legal claim corresponding to a term, or "predicate," that occurs in an authoritative legal source, such as a statute, regulation, or policy, and that is cited in the decision portion of cases. For example, in jurisdictions in which the term "intoxication" occurs in a statute forbidding driving under the influence of alcohol or drugs (DUI), the predicate "intoxication" is an issue, and legal liability depends on whether this predicate is established at trial. "Slurred speech," by contrast, is a "factor" if the decision portion of one or more cases contains findings about "slurred speech" that justify conclusions about the issue of intoxication. This usage differs from Ashley (1991) and others in that our factors are not features developed by domain experts, but rather are classes of factual findings in case decisions denoted by common annotation tags. We surmise that these decision-

Proceedings of the Natural Legal Language Processing Workshop 2019, pages 12–20
Minneapolis, Minesotta, June 7, 2019. ©2019 Association for Computational Linguistics

derived factors are amenable both to HYPO/CATO-like argumentation (Ashley, 1991 and Aleven, 1997) and to alternative machine-learning and inferential techniques.

This paper describes several approaches to lightweight and expedited corpus creation in support of explainable legal decision prediction. The methods are tested on formal written decisions about domain name disputes which are published by the World Intellectual Property Organization (WIPO). The first approach involves human annotators applying a three-layer schema for labeling argument elements, issues, and factors in the panel's findings and decisions on the case. This method is applied to a very small corpus of 25 documents. The second approach is applied to the entire corpus of over 16000 documents and employs a combination of automated preprocessing and human annotation for labeling the outcome for three principal issues in each WIPO case. A third layer of annotation is added by automatically projecting the argument element, issue, and factor annotations onto each sentence in each document of the entire corpus. We are making this a richly annotated corpus available to the research community via MITRE's GitHub space (https://github.com/mitre).

1.1 Prior work

Most early research in automated legal reasoning involved logical representations of legal rules (McCarty 2018). These systems often could justify conclusions in terms of rules, but two factors limited their adoption: (a) the challenges of accurately and scalably formalizing legal rules in computational logic, and (b) the difficulty of matching abstract predicates in rules (e.g., "nuisance") to case facts (e.g., "barking dog").

Research in legal Case-Based Reasoning (CBR) addressed these challenges by reasoning about the similarities and differences between the facts of a given new case and prior cases ("precedents"). The most influential approach to legal CBR involved factor-based argumentation (Ashley, 1991). For example, the CATO system (Aleven, 1997) employed a hierarchy of 26 factors organized into five higher level abstract concepts, or issues. Recent use of the CATO corpus to support

automated identification of factors includes Wyner & Peters (2012) and Wyner (2010), who use GATE Teamware to perform manual annotation of factors. Al-Abdulkarim et al. (2015) annotate both factors and issues in the CATO corpus.

More recently, Sulea et al. (2017) attempted to automatically identify facts in the case description within the top 20 highest ranking bigrams and trigrams as defined by a classification model. While these spans of text were predictive of the area of law, they did not correspond to the facts of the case.

Our objective is a methodology that permits rapid development of explainable predictive systems in new domains. Accordingly, our case features are derived from the justification portion of texts of representative decisions—a readily accessible resource—rather than from the comparatively scarce resource of combined AI and legal expertise. We hypothesize that machine-learning models for deriving these features from the texts of new cases will permit explainable prediction, including both CATO-style factor analysis and other analytical techniques.

2 Data

Disputes over WWW domain name ownership are administrated by the United Nations' World International Property Organization (WIPO), under the Uniform Domain Name Dispute Resolution Policy (UDRP).[1] If a domain name has been previously registered by Party A, and Party B feels that the domain name rightly belongs to them instead, then Party B may file a complaint with WIPO, requesting that the domain name be transferred to them. Party A, the respondent, has the opportunity to respond to the complaint filed by Party B, the complainant. An independent panel of one or more individuals is assigned to review the case and make a ruling. The ruling is published on the WIPO website.[2]

The panel's written decision is divided into multiple sections, including the naming of the parties involved, the domain name(s) in dispute, a summary of the factual background, a summary of the complainant's and respondent's contentions, the panel's discussion of the foregoing information and the panel's legal findings based thereon, and

---

[1] See https://www.icann.org/resources/pages/policy-2012-02-25-en

[2] For example, see , e.g.,
https://www.wipo.int/amc/en/domains/search/text.jsp?case=D2016-1709

finally, the panel's decision on the case overall. Because of the fairly formulaic nature of these documents, they provide a rich source of data for developing automated algorithms that process information about legal issues, factors, and findings. The decision documents are freely downloadable from the WIPO website, with decisions dating back to 2007.

3 Annotation of Argument Elements, Issues and Factors

A key goal of our research is developing a repeatable methodology that permits development of explainable legal prediction systems by agencies that lack the resources to engineer domain-specific feature sets, a process that requires both extensive expertise in the particular legal domain and experience in feature engineering. Instead, our approach requires only the linguistic skills necessary to annotate the decision portion of a representative subset of cases, a much more limited process.

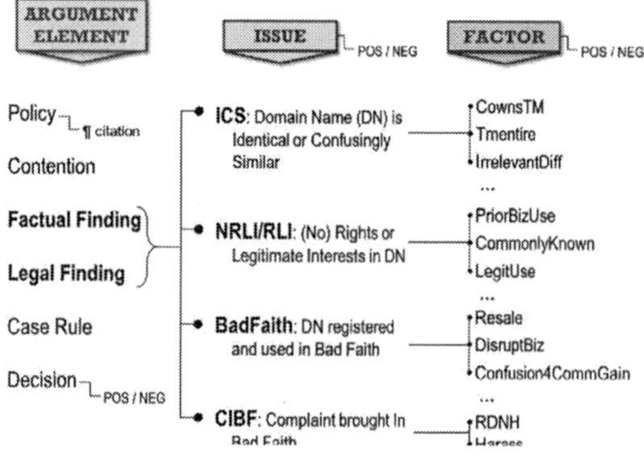

Figure 1: Annotation Scheme for WIPO Decisions

The annotation schema consists of three layers, shown in Figure 1: *Argument Elements*, *Issues*, and *Factors* (sub-issues). The top-layer, Argument Element, consists of six types: Policy, Contention, Factual Finding, Legal Finding, Case Rule, and the Decision on the case as a whole. We have found that with these six argument elements, the majority of sentences within the "Discussion and Findings" and "Decision" sections of WIPO cases can be assigned an argument element label. Each of these argument elements is generally found in all legal

and administrative rulings, so by using these as the anchoring elements of the analysis scheme, our intent is that this approach will have utility in other domains.

We hypothesize that Factual Findings and Legal Findings will have the most predictive and explanatory power. Therefore, Factual Findings and Legal Findings are further categorized according to the *Issue* the panel is addressing. Contentions and Case Rules can also be labelled according to the issue they address.

The Issue tags include the three required elements that the complainant must establish in order to prevail in a WIPO case. These issues are documented in the Uniform Domain Name Dispute Resolution Policy, paragraph 4,[3] and form the backbone of every decision:

(i) ICS: Domain name is Identical or Confusingly Similar to a trademark or service mark in which the complainant has rights.

(ii) NRLI: Respondent has No Rights or Legitimate Interests with respect to the domain name.

(iii) Bad Faith: Domain name has been registered and is being used in Bad Faith.

For element (ii), NRLI, although the dispute is typically approached from the point of view of the complainant demonstrating that the respondent has no RLI (i.e., NRLI), it is very often the case that the panel considers evidence in support of the rights or legitimate interests of the Respondent. In that case, RLI is available as an issue tag.

In addition, the domain name resolution procedure allows for situations in which the complainant abuses the process by filing the complaint in bad faith (CIBF).[4]

Each of these issues can be further sub-categorized according to *Factors*, a sampling of which is shown in Figure 1. Factors are the elements which we hypothesize will prove most useful for explainable legal prediction. For example, whether or not the complainant owns rights in the trademark (CownsTM) is a critical factor in establishing the outcome of the first issue about the confusability of the domain name and trademark. In our annotation scheme, there are eight factors for the ICS issue, four factors for

---

[3] https://www.icann.org/resources/pages/policy-2012-02-25-en#4

[4] see See 15(e) of the Rules for Uniform Domain Name Dispute Resolution Policy for CIBF,

https://www.icann.org/resources/pages/udrp-rules-2015-03-11-en

Case No	Text	Annotation
D2012-1430	in two instances the TURBOFIRE mark has been reproduced in a domain name, utilizing a dash "-" between the "turbo" and "fire" portion of the mark, which the Panel disregards as irrelevant under this element of the Policy	FACTUAL_FINDING-ICS-IrrelevantDiff
D2012-1430	The Panel thus finds that the disputed domain names are confusingly similar to the Complainant's registered trademarks	LEGAL_FINDING-ICS
D2012-1430	Additionally, as several of the disputed domain names are used to host online shopping websites offering products similar to those of the Complainant, from which the Respondent presumably generates revenue,	FACTUAL_FINDING-NRLI-LegitUse subissue-polarity=negative
D2012-1430	the Respondent clearly is not making any noncommercial or fair use of those domain names	LEGAL_FINDING-NRLI-LegitUse subissue-polarity=negative
D2012-1430	…the Respondent is clearly attempting to divert Internet traffic intended for the Complainant's website to its own for commercial gain by creating a likelihood of confusion as to the source or sponsorship of the Respondent's websites and products.	FACTUAL_FINDING-BadFaith-Confusion4CommGain
D2012-1430	Such use constitutes bad faith under paragraph 4(b)(iv) of the Policy.	LEGAL_FINDING-BadFaith-Confusion4CommGain
D2016-0534	The Complainant must have been aware that the Disputed Domain Name existed when it chose to register its UNIKS trademark.	FACTUAL_FINDING-CIBF-RDNH
D2016-0534	Taking into account all of the above the Panel has no hesitation in finding that the present case amounts to RDNH by the Complainant.	LEGAL_FINDING-CIBF-RDNH

Table 1: Example Annotations from WIPO Decisions

NRLI/RLI, and seven for BadFaith. Some of the factors are derived from the WIPO policy and some were discovered in a pilot annotation phase. For CIBF, two factor tags are available: RDNH (Reverse Domain Name Hijacking) and Harass (complaint brought primarily to harass DN holder).

Each level of annotation also has an "Other" option (not shown in Figure 1) to accommodate semantics that are not covered by the predefined tags, and there is a free-form Comment field which the annotator can use to capture ad hoc labels and enter notes.

A Citation attribute is used to capture the paragraph citation of Policy references, when they are explicitly made in the text. We plan to explore the citations as predictive features in future research. Finally, a Polarity attribute is used to capture positive/negative values for Decisions, Issues, and Factors.

Our three-layered annotation approach of labeling Argument Elements, Issues, and Factors relies on having clear divisions between the facts, the decision, and the decision justification. Aletras et al. (2016) found that the facts section of the case text provided the best predictors of case decision. It is our hypothesis that this methodology will be particularly useful in domains with a specific set of issues and justifications, for example, granting government benefits, or tenant/landlord disputes.

Table 1 shows eight typical annotations. Tags are preferentially applied to clauses and sentences, as opposed to shorter units such as noun phrases, in order to identify the complete linguistic proposition corresponding to the annotation label.

The MITRE Annotation Toolkit (MAT) is used to perform the annotation.[5] A screenshot is shown in Figure 2, illustrating the cascading menus that give the annotator quick access to the entire tag hierarchy.

3.1 Inter-Annotator Agreement

The manual annotation was performed by two individuals, who, while experienced in the creation of annotated corpora for developing natural language processing systems, have no formal training in the legal domain. Before performing the double annotation used for agreement measures, annotation guidelines were written and a set of six practice documents was identified, three with a positive outcome (the domain name was transferred to the complainant) and three with a

---

[5] Available for download at http://mat-annotation.sourceforge.net/

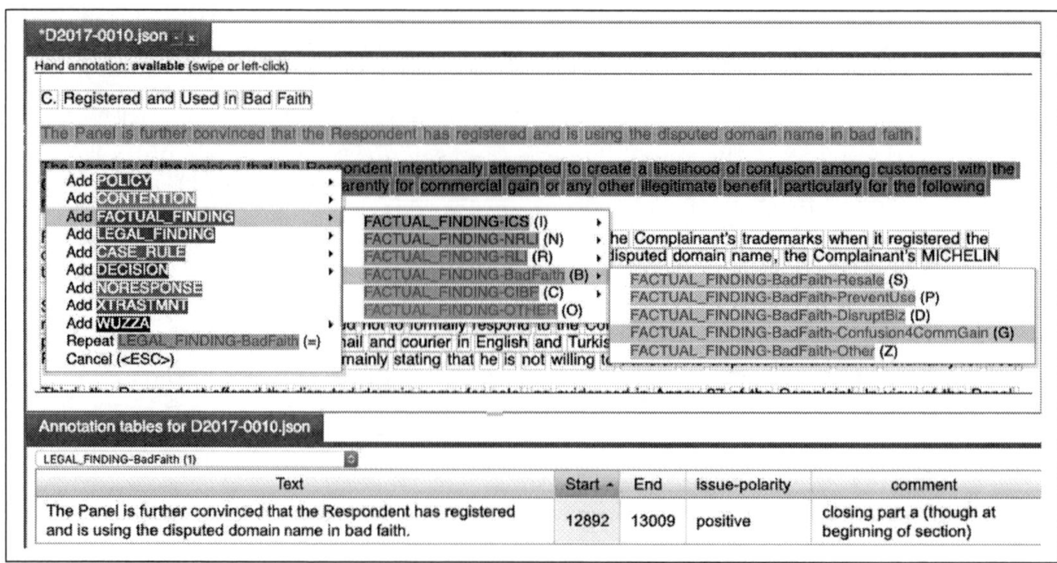

Figure 2: MITRE Annotation Tool (MAT)

negative outcome. These were doubly annotated in three trial phases, with the annotators meeting after each pair of documents to discuss differences and clarify the guidelines. Once the practice phase was complete, additional double-annotation was performed on a different set of six documents, which yielded 232 annotations. Agreement was measured on these annotations. Table 2 presents the inter-annotator agreement results, reported as percent agreement using Cohen's Kappa calculation (Cohen, 1960) vs. the raw agreement, shown in parentheses. As there were only two annotators, we do not compute inter-annotator agreement comparisons in a pair-wise fashion, i.e., for each annotator separately.

	Argument Element	Issue	Factor	Factor Normalized for Other vs. Nil
All Argument Element Types	75% (80%)	80% (85%)	68% (76%)	74% (84%)
Only Legal Findings & Factual Findings	57% (78%)	80% (86%)	69% (74%)	75% (83%)

Table 2: Inter-Annotator Agreement (Kappa vs. Raw)

Overall, the agreement was 75% on argument elements, 80% on issues, and 68% on factors. For Legal Findings and Factual Findings – features which we hypothesize will have greater predictive and explainable power – the levels of agreement on this set of six documents was lower for argument elements, at 57%, and did not differ significantly for issues and factors. We observed that one difference that lowers agreement occurs when one annotator chooses to specify "Other" as a factor label and the other annotator opts to not set a factor label at all (an alternative that is allowed by the guidelines). It is quite subjective whether the semantics of the clause warrant an "Other" factor label or no label. If we normalize the difference, allowing Other and Nil to be equivalant, the agreement on factors increases from 68% to 74% on all argument element tags and from 69% to 75% on Legal Findings and Factual Findings.

The WIPO administrative decisions exhibit a fair amount of variability in terms of clarity when it comes to assigning argument elements, issues, and factor labels. For example, on some subsets of files, the two annotators were able to achieve raw agreement as high as 99% on the Issue labels for Legal Findings and Factual Findings. We found that for the majority of cases that were doubly annotated, agreement was higher on the Legal Findings and Factual Findings than across all argument element types, a fact that is not reflected in Table 2, which contains totals for all documents that were doubly annotated. Thus, although some cases are more challenging to annotate than others, overall the quantitative results indicate that the task is tractable for non-legal experts.

3.2 Predicting Decisions from Mapped Tags

From the small set of 25 annotated documents (0.14% of the entire corpus), we are able to project the annotations to similar sentences throughout the entire corpus of documents.

This projection is accomplished through the use of word and sentence embeddings to find text that is semantically similar to the annotated text. The accuracy of mapped tags as predictive features depends on both the annotation conventions and the details of the clustering. An initial evaluation of adequacy and correctness of these initial two steps can performed by determining the predictive accuracy of the mapped tags. If the tags are capturing the actual decision, then a high degree of accuracy should be achievable by training a model that predicts overall case decisions, or decisions for individual issues, from the mapped tags.

The projection method is as follows. Word embeddings are trained on the tokenized corpus using FastText (Mikolov, 2018). FastText computes embeddings for character n-grams and then sums the character n-gram embeddings to compute the embedding for a word. The character embeddings are computed using a method similar to Word2Vec (Mikolov, 2013). FastText is beneficial for rare words, morphologically rich languages and smaller corpora. This yields one vector per token that captures the semantics of the word through the surrounding context.

The resulting word embeddings are then used to compute sentence embeddings by averaging the vectors of the words in each sentence for each of the 2.64 million sentences in our corpus. Next, these word embeddings are used to compute sentence embeddings by averaging the vectors of the words in each sentence for each of the 2.64 million sentences in our corpus. Semantically similar sentences are close to each other in semantic-embedding space. A notable limitation of this approach is that sentences that are lexically very similar but that have opposite polarity are often very close in this embedding space. An example is simple negation via "not," for example "the panel finds that it was properly constituted" and "the panel finds that it was not properly constituted" differ by a single word but have opposite legal effects. We attempted to compensate for this limitation by incorporating polarity annotations into the projected tags. The annotation convention was the polarity attribute was assumed to be "positive" if not explicitly annotated. Out of

890 annotations, 173 (19.4%) contained negative polarity and 717 contained positive polarity. The polarity attribute was extracted for each annotation and incorporated into the projected tag. The sentences are then clustered into 512 clusters by their embeddings. The clusters establish neighborhoods of similar sentences.

Once the word embeddings have been trained, embeddings for the annotation spans of text are trained using the same method as was used to compute sentence embeddings. While the annotation spans are not strictly sentences, the sentence embedding method can be used to compute embeddings of arbitrary spans of text.

Once the word embeddings, corpus sentence embeddings, annotation span embeddings and clusters have been computed, the tags can be projected. For each annotation label of interest for the specific experiment, we retrieve the top 10,000 sentences in the corpus ranked by cosine similarity to the annotated spans. Then, the annotation label is projected to each cluster associated with each retrieved sentence.

For these prediction tasks, we do not use the words of the sentences. Instead, we use the cluster label of each sentence in the document. The sentences are selected according to task-specific criteria. XGBoost (Chen and Guestrin, 2016), an efficient implementation of gradient boosted machines, is used in all prediction tasks in this work. These are preliminary results, and we continue to iterate to improve the outcomes.

As the outcome decision labels are highly skewed, 91% positive (14591 cases), 9% negative (1407 cases), we do not create a dedicated test set. Instead, we opt for 10 random test/train splits and report the average area under the curve (AUC), and per class precision, recall and F1 score micro-averaged over the 10 trials.

In a separate paper (Branting et al., 2019) we report on several experiments that make use of the projected tags. As proof of concept for the methodology described in this paper, we report only on the results for predicting case outcomes. The results are preliminary, intended solely to demonstrate the feasibility of the approach.

This experiment used the tag projection method described above, and retrieved sentences based on all annotation types. This method selected 1.8M sentences out of the total corpus of 2.6M. Predicting overall case outcome with the annotated data gave strong results with an average AUC of

78.5% and a standard deviation of 0.01. The positive class, the majority class in this dataset, earned a 90% F1 (97% precision and 83.9% recall). The negative class was lower with a 42.9% F1 (30.4% precision, 73.1% recall). This experiment indicates that tags mapped from a modest set of annotated cases are sufficient to express the decisions in the Findings section.

4 Annotation of legal rulings on issue outcome in WIPO Decisions

In a WIPO case, the complainant needs to prevail in each of the three primary issues – ICS, NRLI, and Bad Faith – in order for there to be a positive outcome, i.e., the domain name is transferred to the complainant. Being able to accurately identify the outcome of each issue is therefore useful in predicting the outcome of the case overall. Issue-level outcomes take the form of legal findings (e.g., see the second row in Table 1), and are typically found within easily identifiable sub-sections of the panel's decision. They often appear as the last sentence in the issue-level sub-sections – a pattern we were able to exploit, but only to a limited degree, as described below. The manner in which the legal finding is stated varies as well. As a result, a fully automated approach to issue-level outcome annotation was not possible, and manually annotating the corpus would be prohibitively time consuming for the entire set of over 48000 issue outcomes (16000 cases x 3). We therefore used a multi-step interactive approach to annotate the issue outcomes, described next.

Approximately 90% of the cases have a positive outcome, so the first step was to automatically annotate positive cases with a positive outcome for each of the three issues. This left 10% of the cases that have a negative overall outcome, and which could potentially have negative outcomes in one, two, or all three of the issues – up to approximately 5000 issue outcomes in total. In those cases where the sub-section on an issue could not be automatically located in the panel's decision, it was temporally labelled as having a missing value for the issue outcome. A few hundred Bad Faith issue outcomes were manually annotated before it was deemed to take too long.

Next, we extracted all the unique last sentences in the issue-level subsections still missing an outcome annotation. This gave us approximately 3000 sentences which we manually annotated with one of the following values:

- True (positive outcome for the issue)

- False (negative outcome for the issue)

- No_Decision (The panel asserts that it does not need to make a decision on this issue because some other issue has a negative outcome.)

- ? (does not describe an outcome)

The manual annotation revealed some discrepancies which needed to be corrected, for example, cases with an overall positive outcome that had issues with a negative outcome and issue outcomes appearing outside their designated subsection.

Table 3 summarizes the current state of the issue-level annotation for the WIPO corpus of 16024 cases.

Issue	TRUE	FALSE	NO_DECISION	Total With Value		No Value	
				Number	Percent	Number	Total Cases
ICS	15571	139	158	15868	99%	156	16024
NRLI	14762	432	598	15792	99%	232	16024
BadFaith	14615	531	412	15558	97%	466	16024
TOTALS	44948	1102	1168	47218		854	

Table 3: Issue-Level Outcome Annotations

Between 97% and 99% of the corpus has been annotated for issue-level outcomes, depending on the issue, with 845 issue outcomes yet to be resolved.

For those cases that could not be annotated as True, False, or No_Decision, we are currently in the process of analyzing additional patterns that can be exploited automatically. We are also performing additional automated quality control checks that look for inconsistencies, e.g., the overall case outcome being false, but none of the issues are false.

In this section we have described a methodology for annotating a large corpus for issue-level decisions. While the exact approach is necessarily dependent on specifics that are unique to the WIPO domain, our expectation is that it is generalizable to other datasets. For instance, not all legal and administrative rulings have clearly identifiable case-level decisions, but when they do, they can be automatically extracted and then used to infer issue-level decision values. Other prototypical patterns can be used to automate the annotation, and the more complicated texts can be reserved for human review.

4.1 Issue-Outcome Prediction

We have begun experimenting with the issue-level outcome annotation, testing different machine-learning approaches for predicting issue outcomes based on these annotated sentences. The task is to predict whether a given sentence favors the respondent (a negative outcome), favors the complainant (a positive outcome), or states that the panel is not making a decision for this issue. A subset of the corpus was divided into 1438 training samples and 709 test samples. The best performance achieved thus far has been from an approach utilizing a 300-dimensional Word Embedding from FastText, with 1 million word vectors trained on Wikipedia in 2017 (Mikolov, 2017). Results are shown in Table 4.

	Precision	Recall	F1
Negative Outcome	0.89	0.95	0.92
Positive Outcome	0.96	0.93	0.94
No_Decision	0.98	0.93	0.95

Table 4: Issue-Level Prediction Scores

5 Conclusions and Future Work

Computational techniques for explainable legal problem solving have existed for many years, but broad adoption of these techniques has been impeded by their requirement for manual feature labeling. The rise of large-scale text analytics and machine learning promised a way to finesse this obstacle, but the limited explanatory capability of these approaches has limited their adoption in law where decisions must be justified in terms of authoritative legal sources.

This paper has described three approaches to exploiting minimalist knowledge engineering in the form of an extremely small corpus annotated by non-legal experts and using that annotation and regularities discernible in the data to automatically augment and extend these annotations. We have provided proof-of-concept of the quality and utility of these annotations by reporting preliminary results on issue-level and case-level decision prediction algorithms.

We anticipate that the accuracy of annotation projection can be improved by use of improved embeddings methods. Since this work has started, very large pre-trained language models have been released, including ELMO (Peters, 2018), BERT (Devlin, 2018) and GPT-2 (Radford, 2019). Future work should use these pre-trained models to create embeddings for sentences and annotations to improve the tag projection. These embedding algorithms capture greater nuance of language than FastText/Word2Vec (possibly including word sense), and their pre-trained models are built from massive data collections processed on massive compute clusters.

In future work, the domains of particular interest to us include disability benefit claims, immigration petitions, landlord-tenant disputes, and attorney misconduct complaints. The high volumes of these types of cases mean that large training sets are available and that agencies have an incentive to consider technologies to improve decision processes. We anticipate applying the annotation methodologies described in this paper to an administrative agency starting in the next few months, which will provide a more realistic evaluation of its ability to support system development in the service of actual agency decision making.

Acknowledgments

We would like to thank the anonymous reviewers for their feedback and suggestions.

References

Al-Abdulkarim, Latifa, Katie Atkinson, and Trevor Bench-Capon. 2015. Factors, Issues and Values: Revisiting Reasoning with Cases. In *Proceedings of the 15th International Conference on Artificial intelligence and Law* (pp. 3-12). ACM.

Aletras, Nikolaos, Dimitrios Tsarapatsanis, Daniel Preoţiuc-Pietro, and Vasileios Lampos. 2016. Predicting Judicial Decisions of the European Court of Human Rights: A Natural Language Processing Perspective. *PeerJ Computer Science* 2: e93. https://peerj.com/articles/cs-93/ .

Aleven, Vincent. 1997. *Teaching Case-Based Argumentation Through a Model and Examples*. Ph.D. thesis, University of Pittsburgh.

Aleven, Vincent. 2003. Using Background Knowledge in Case-based Legal Reasoning: a Computational Model and an Intelligent Learning Environment. *Artificial Intelligence* 150.1-2: 183-237.

Ashley, Kevin D. 1991. *Modeling Legal Arguments: Reasoning with Cases and Hypotheticals*. MIT Press.

Branting, Karl, Craig Pfeifer, Lisa Ferro, Alex Yeh, Brandy Weiss, Mark Pfaff, Amartya Chakraborty, and Bradford Brown. 2019. Semi-supervised Methods for Explainable Legal Prediction. To appear, *Proceedings of the 19th International*

Conference on AI and Law (ICAIL 2019), Montreal, Canada, June 17-21, 2019.

Chen, Tianqi, and Carlos Guestrin. 2016. XGBoost: A scalable tree boosting system. In *Proceedings of the 22nd ACM SIGKDD International Conference on Knowledge Discovery and Data Mining*, pp. 785-794. http://arxiv.org/abs/1603.02754.

Cohen, Jacob. 1960. A coefficient of agreement for nominal scales. *Educational and Psychological Measurement*, 20, pp. 37-47.

Devlin, Jacob, Ming-Wei Chang, Kenton Lee and Kristina Toutanova. 2018. BERT: Pre-training of Deep Bidirectional Transformers for Language Understanding. *CoRR abs/1810.04805 (2018)*.

Katz, Daniel Martin, Michael J. Bommarito II, and Josh Blackman. 2017. A General Approach for Predicting the Behavior of the Supreme Court of the United States. *PloS One*, 12:4.

McCarty, L. Thorne. 2018. Finding the right balance in Artificial Intelligence and Law. In *Research Handbook on the Law of Artificial Intelligence*, Edward Elgar Publishing.

Medvedeva, Masha, Michel Vols, and Martijn Wieling. 2018. Judicial Decisions of the European Court of Human Rights: Looking into the Crystal Ball. In *Proceedings of the Conference on Empirical Legal Studies*.

Mikolov, Tomas, Edouard Grave, Piotr Bojanowski, Christian Puhrsch, and Armand Joulin. 2017. Advances in Pre-training Distributed Word Representations. In *Proceedings of the Eleventh International Conference on Language Resources and Evaluation (LREC-2018)*, pp. 52-55. http://aclweb.org/anthology/L18-1008.

Mikolov, Tomas, Ilya Sutskever, Kai Chen, Greg S. Corrado and Jeffrey Dean. 2013. Distributed Representations of Words and Phrases and their Compositionality. In *Advances in Neural Information Processing Systems*, pp. 3111-3119.

Peters, Matthew E., Mark Neumann, Mohit Iyyer, Matt Gardner, Christopher Clark, Kenton Lee and Luke S. Zettlemoyer. 2018. Deep Contextualized Word Representations. In *Proceedings of NAACL-HLT*, pp. 2227-2237. https://aclweb.org/anthology/N18-1202

Radford, Alec, Jeff Wu, Rewon Child, David Luan, Dario Amodei, Ilya Sutskever. 2019. Language Models are Unsupervised Multitask Learners.

Sulea, Octavia-Maria, Marcos Zampieri, Mihaela Vela and Josef van Genabith. 2017. Predicting the Law Area and Decisions of French Supreme Court Cases. In *Proceedings of the International Conference on Recent Advances in Natural Language Processing (RANLP 2017)*, pp. 716-722. https://aclweb.org/anthology/papers/R/R17/R17-1092/

Wyner, Adam, and Wim Peters. 2012. Semantic Annotations for Legal Text Processing using GATE Teamware. In *Semantic Processing of Legal Texts (SPLeT-2012) Workshop Programme*, p. 34.

Wyner, Adam Z. 2010. Towards Annotating and Extracting Textual Legal Case Elements. In *Informatica e Diritto: Special Issue on Legal Ontologies and Artificial Intelligent Techniques* 19.1-2: 9-18.

The Extent of Repetition in Contract Language

Dan Simonson
BlackBoiler LLC
Arlington, VA 22207
dan.simonson@blackboiler.com

Daniel Broderick
BlackBoiler LLC
Arlington, VA 22207
dan@blackboiler.com

Jonathan Herr
BlackBoiler LLC
Arlington, VA 22207
jonathan@blackboiler.com

Abstract

Contract language is repetitive (Anderson and Manns, 2017), but so is all language (Zipf, 1949). In this paper, we measure the extent to which contract language in English is repetitive compared with the language of other English language corpora. Contracts have much smaller vocabulary sizes compared with similarly sized non-contract corpora across multiple contract types, contain $1/5^{th}$ as many hapax legomena, pattern differently on a log-log plot, use fewer pronouns, and contain sentences that are about 20% more similar to one another than in other corpora. These suggest that the study of contracts in natural language processing controls for some linguistic phenomena and allows for more in depth study of others.

1 Introduction

Among attorneys and those in the legal professions, contract language is considered "repetitive," but the same can be said about natural language in general (Zipf, 1949). Anderson and Manns (2017) largely attribute the repetitive nature of contract language to drafting methodologies. Attorneys rarely start contracts or provisions from a blank document. Anderson and Manns (2017) showed that attorneys typically select a precedent contracts and fit them to the parameters of a new relationship with a counterparty. The same is true when an attorney drafts a new contract provision, beginning with an old provision from an existing agreement. As a result, new or novel language is infrequent as compared to other kinds of natural language. They assessed these similarities using Levenshtein distance, which is somewhat unusual with respect to the methods and statistics typically used in natural language processing and corpus linguistics, and they did not compare their corpus of contracts against data of the sort typically used in natural language processing and corpus linguistics—for our purposes, the Brown Corpus (Francis and Kučera, 1964, 1971, 1979) and Wikipedia (King, 2018). This paper seeks to describe quantitatively the extent to which contract language is more repetitive than the language found in these corpora.

We aim this paper at multiple audiences. Our own motivation was to more deeply understand the driving linguistic and distributional factors behind technology that Broderick et al. (2016) developed, and we hope those in industry who work with or are evaluating legal technology can read this work to understand how this repetition uniquely supports the automation of work involving contract language. We hope the computational linguist working on contract or legal texts can use the findings here to justify certain decisions and positions made in their own work, as a basic foundation of facts can help reduce exponentially the tree of decisions made in practice. We hope the computational linguistics community at large can take from this paper that contract language has properties advantageous for problems that prefer more constrained—but still natural—language.

In this paper, we present analyses of contract language in English, juxtaposing them against two other English language corpora. In Section (2), we discuss prior work toward this end. In Section (3), we discuss the data used in this study: a set of contract corpora containing 1,737 documents and two baseline corpora for comparison. In Section (4), we discuss the distribution of tokens in our contract corpus compared with the baseline corpora and look more closely at the data to affirm the meaning of those distributions. In Section (5), we step up from the token level to look at similarity at the sentential level through a nearest neighbors analysis. In Sections (6 & 7), we discuss these findings broadly and conclude.

Proceedings of the Natural Legal Language Processing Workshop 2019, pages 21–30
Minneapolis, Minesotta, June 7, 2019. ©2019 Association for Computational Linguistics

2 Prior Work

Numerous studies have been done on contract corpora, many with specific ends in mind. Faber and Lauridsen (1991) prepared a corpus referred to as the "Danish-English-French corpus in contract law," or the "Aarhus corpus" (Curtotti and McCreath, 2011). This corpus contains both contracts and legal literature, sampling what language was available at the time for study, and containing 776 pages of contracts, likely around 400,000 tokens.[1] A few corpus studies have been conducted previously. Blom and Trosborg (1992) look at speech acts in the Danish-English-French corpus and how different speech acts create the relationship established between two parties in a contract, as well as other types of legal language. Nielsen and Wichmann (1994) look at the English subcorpus of the Danish-English-French corpus of a size of around 50,000 tokens in conjunction with an equally sized corpus of their own creation in German, focused primarily on how obligation is expressed in both languages. Anesa (2007) examine a corpus of 12 contracts (50,828 tokens) in English to codify the linguistic strategies used to make certain provisions vague while others specific, particularly because contracts are rarely written from scratch, and vague provisions have broad applicability when cut-and-paste between contracts. Carvalho (2008) and Mohammad et al. (2010) both built parallel corpora for the purposes of improving contract translation between English and Brazilian Portuguese and Arabic respectively. Most extensively, Curtotti and McCreath (2011) conducted a study of a corpus of Australian English contracts, examining the distribution and statistics of a corpus of 256 contracts. They primarily focused on demonstrating that the corpus they had collected was representative, presenting numerous statistics to that end. Anderson and Manns (2017) collected a corpus of 12,407 agreements with the end of showing precedent relationships using Levenshtein distance and clustering. Their goal was not to analyze the properties of contract language itself, but to show explicitly how contracts are copied from one another.

Studies have also been done on repetitive, conventionalized language use more broadly. Halliday (1988) examined the historical development of conventionalized language use in the sciences, demonstrating qualitatively that science developed a rhetorical style using already existing rhetorical elements of English in a way most relevant to the experimental style of the physical sciences. Extensive corpus work has looked at the physical sciences to better understand the linguistic processes of used to create and frame understanding in scientific work (Argamon et al., 2005) and to exploit the repetitive nature of such documents to find phrases that are more information-laden than their more conventionalized counterparts (Degaetano-Ortlieb and Teich, 2017).

3 Data

In this section, we describe the data used in this study, both the contracts we gathered for analysis and the baseline corpora used to contrast the contract corpus.

3.1 Contract Corpus

Our subject matter expert gathered a corpus of contracts. They selected categories and recovered documents relevant to those categories through search engines and from EDGAR,[2] issuing queries based on phrases indicative of particular contract types, and selecting contracts that they considered, as an expert, to be of the specific contract type.

Our subject matter expert searched for five types of contracts. Prime Contracts are an agreement between a project owner and a general contractor. Subcontracts are between a general contractor and a subcontractor or trade contractor for specific subcomponents of a project, such as implementing the drywall in the building. Non-Disclosure Agreements are agreements related to the exchange of information and the confidential treatment thereof. Purchase Orders is an agreement for the purchase of products between a buyer and a seller. Services Agreements is an agreement for one party to supply another party with a service. Prime Contracts and Subcontracts were selected with relation to the construction industry; the other types were selected more broadly.

Contracts identified with formatting issues due to failed optical character recognition (OCR) were removed. This filtering process was not perfect, however, as some OCR errors remain in the data.

---

[1] We were not able to obtain access to this corpus, and are estimating this based on the provided page count (Faber and Lauridsen, 1991) at 500 tokens per page.

[2] EDGAR is a service of the United States Securities and Exchange Commission: (https://www.sec.gov/edgar.shtml)

To some extent, we have to acknowledge that some noise in contract data is inevitable; there are no universal standards for the interchange of contract documents. Further, while the contracts retrieved represent unique agreements, they themselves are not necessarily unique. This is intended to represent the typical distribution and content of contract documents exchanged on a regular basis. Table (1) contains the results of this retrieval process, a total of 1,737 documents containing a total of over 15 million tokens.

To find tokens and sentence boundaries, corpora were pre-processed with SpaCy (Honnibal and Johnson, 2015).[3]

Table 1: Document and Token Counts per Category.

Category	# docs	# tokens	toks/doc
NDAs	791	1,955,522	2,472
Prime Contracts	174	5,417,987	31,138
Purchase Order	229	1,933,547	8,443
Service Agreements	137	1,216,724	8,881
Subcontracts	406	5,029,433	12,388
Total	1,737	15,553,213	8,954

3.2 Baseline Corpora

We compare the contract corpora against two others: Wikipedia and the Brown Corpus.

For Wikipedia, we used King (2018)'s release of the encyclopedia on Kaggle. This was pre-processed with most mark-up removed and put into a SQLite database for easy accessibility and reproducibility, containing 4,902,648 articles. While the database is organized on a section-by-section basis, we retrieve all text article-by-article to mirror how we access contract documents.

The Brown Corpus (Brown) is a representative corpus of American English (Francis and Kučera, 1964, 1971, 1979). As the first digital corpus of natural language, the Brown Corpus has acted as a common litmus test across experimental configurations for decades. While more contemporary corpora exist (Mair, 1997; Davies, 2010), Brown is much easier to access, and while specific lexical items themselves may have changed over the last sixty years, we do not anticipate that the relative distribution of lexical items in the English language itself to have changed dramatically in that time. "fileids" are considered document boundaries; these are in some cases subsamples of whole documents. Brown was used through the interface provided by NLTK (Bird et al., 2009).[4]

To find tokens and sentence boundaries, corpora were pre-processed with SpaCy (Honnibal and Johnson, 2015).[5] This includes the Brown Corpus, which was re-tokenized to be consistent with the other corpora.

4 Rank-Counts Analysis

In this section, we present an analysis of the rank-vs-counts curves of the corpora analyzed. Often referred to as a *Zipfian* analysis, we counted the frequency of each token type and arranged the counts by their respective ranks—that is, the most frequent word has a rank of 1, the second most frequent word has a rank of 2. Natural language corpora approximately exhibit *Zipf's Law* (Zipf, 1949; Manning and Schütze, 1999)—that a word's frequency is inversely proportional to its rank ($f \propto r^{-1}$). This distribution is difficult to observe on a linear plot and is better observed on a log-log plot, where it appears linear.

For maximum comparability, we subsampled our corpora to the number of tokens in the smallest corpus, rounded up to the nearest document. In other words, we included one whole document at a time until we were just in excess of the number of tokens in the smallest corpus—in this case, the Brown Corpus with 1,161,192 tokens.

4.1 Results

Figure (1) contains a log-log plot of the rank-vs-counts for each word type in the subcorpora counted. Notably, the rank-counts curve of the contract corpus bends downward around rank 1000. This bend was also previously identified in Curtotti and McCreath (2011), who chose to justify that this deviation is normal for typical English language corpora. This is true, but juxtaposing the curves for the contracts and baseline corpora reveals that the curves of the contract subcorpora are far steeper. This means that there are far fewer rare word types in the contract corpora than in the baseline corpora—in other words, that rare words appear less often in contracts.

Inspection of the statistics describing the curves is more revealing. Table (2)[6] presents these val-

---

[3] https://spacy.io/

[4] https://www.nltk.org/data.html

[5] https://spacy.io/

[6] We included TTR largely as a matter of convention and since the number of tokens in each sampled subcorpus is similar.

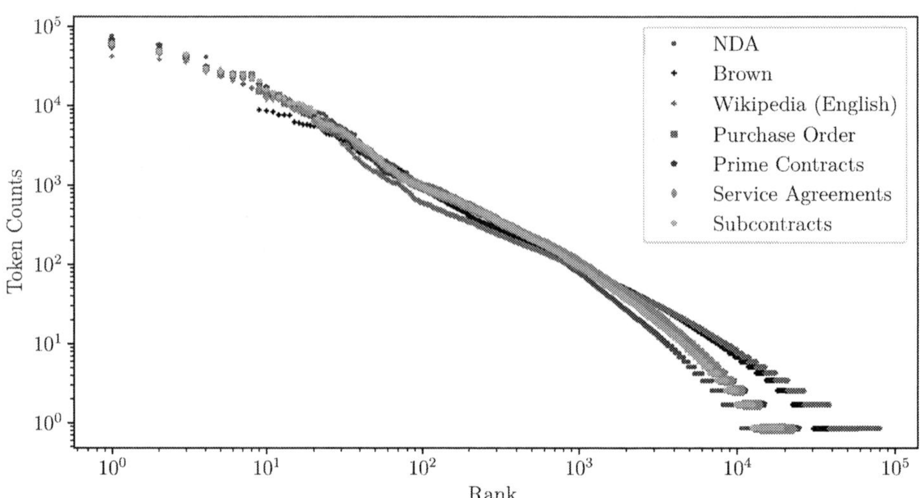

Figure 1: Log-log plots of rank vs frequency of tokens in each contract subcorpus and the baseline corpora.

Table 2: Raw Statistics on Subsamples of Corpora Investigated. $|C|$ indicates the size of the whole corpus; $|S|$ indicates the size of the subcorpus investigated.

Series	$|C|$	$|S|$	# Tokens	# Types	TTR	# Hapax	H/Types	H/Tokens
Brown	500	500	1,161,192	56,057	4.83%	25,559	45.59%	2.20%
Wikipedia:EN	4.9M	1,559	1,161,264	78,973	6.80%	40,820	51.69%	3.52%
NDA	791	484	1,164,051	17,454	1.50%	6,837	39.17%	0.59%
Purchase Order	229	132	1,164,421	21,670	1.86%	8,404	38.78%	0.72%
Prime Contracts	174	36	1,162,939	23,971	2.06%	9,461	39.47%	0.81%
Services Agreements	137	131	1,164,687	22,854	1.96%	8,915	39.01%	0.77%
Subcontracts	406	96	1,163,421	19,052	1.64%	6,670	35.01%	0.57%

ues, which exhibit a clear distinction between the baseline corpora and the contract corpora by all measures. The number of word types is more than double at the least extreme, Prime Contracts vs Brown, and is pentupled at the extreme, NDAs vs Wikipedia. These differences make sense. Prime Contracts are the most likely to be negotiated and tailored to the specific deal while NDAs are the least likely to be nitpicked, themselves often a preliminary step to generating the larger, revenue-generating deal.

The extreme case of a rare item is what is commonly referred to as a *hapax legomena*: a word that is only contained once in a corpus and never seen again. These are visible in Figure (1) toward the bottom right—the final "stair step" as the counts approach zero. Another measure to further illuminate the difference between the baseline and contract corpora is the ratio between the number of hapax legomena and the number of tokens in the corpus. Hapax / Tokens tells us "out of all the words we see in the corpus, how often do we encounter a word that we have never seen before and never see again." As fractions, for Brown, this ratio is 1/35; that is, every 35th word we see once, and never again. For Wikipedia, it is about 1/24.

For NDAs, the Hapax / Tokens ratio is 1/135; for Prime Contracts, the ratio is around 1/120. Between the Prime Contracts and Wikipedia, this difference is nearly 1/5—that is, for every 5 hapax legomena in the Wikipedia corpus, there is 1 in the Prime Contracts corpus. Extremely rare word types—hapax legomena—do not appear in contracts as often as in Brown or Wikipedia.

4.2 Qualitative Inspection

This section presents the content of the corpora studied to validate, from a qualitative perspective, the patterns identified quantitatively. Specifically, we examine both of these sorts of items to give qualitative context to the statistics given in Section (4.1), understanding what these differences mean for a rare, open class of types (hapax legomena, Section 4.2.1) and a frequent, closed class of types (pronouns, Section 4.2.2).

4.2.1 Hapax Legomena

As discussed in Section (4), the corpora diverge with respect to the frequency of rare tokens in the corpora, particularly with respect to the number of hapax legomena. To further illuminate the nature of these, Table (3) contains examples of hapax legomena from each subcorpus.

Based on the given samples, we can see that in both cases, the hapax legomena are often numbers or proper nouns. The contract corpora are also more susceptible to generally noisy data. The use of capitalization for emphasis differentiated a lot of terms that otherwise appear frequently (e.g. "INTRODUCTION"), as well as unique numbering schemes (e.g. "FP-1"). Additionally, though despite our efforts to remove data in which OCR failed, a few examples slipped through of (e.g. "wri+en" and "totheChangeinwriting").

Given these differences, we suspect further improvements, such as using lemmas and more carefully removing OCR errors, would actually amplify the difference in numbers of hapax legomena between corpora. Wikipedia's are mostly proper nouns, so these would remain hapax legomena—even lemmatized—while many in the contract subcorpora would be lemmatized into another word or removed from the data entirely. These modifications will amplify whatever differences were observed in this experimental configuration.

4.2.2 Frequency and Use of Pronouns

In some ways, pronouns—words such as "she," "their," and "itself"—are the reverse of hapax legomena, often being amongst the most common words in a corpus. However, they too appear less often in contracts. In both baseline corpora, 73,521 pronouns appeared, while in the contract corpora, a combined 52,764 pronouns appeared despite being 2.5 times larger than the combined baseline corpora. This is presumably to achieve precision and reduce ambiguity, as pronouns are often ambiguous and must be determined from context, but not all pronouns pattern alike.

The log frequency ratio shows these differences quite well. We define the log frequency ratio in this case to be $LF_{a,b}(w) = \log_{10} \frac{f_a(w)}{f_b(w)}$, where a and b are corpora, w is a token type, and $f_a(w)$ is the frequency of token type w in corpus a. Intuitively, if $LF_{a,b}(w)$ is zero, w appears with equal frequency in a and b; if it is negative, w appears more often in b. With log base 10, $LF_{a,b}(w) = 1.0$ means w appeared in corpus a 10 times as often as in b, etc. We will refer to all contract corpora as C_c and all baseline corpora as C_b. *forms of x* include the nominative, accusative, reflexive, and possessive forms of the pronouns—so *forms of "they"* include "they," "them," "their," and "themselves."

Forms of "he" and "she" appear the most com-

Table 3: Examples of Hapax Legomena From the Subcorpora Analyzed.

Corpus	Sample of Hapax Legomena Tokens
Brown	'ARF', 'Piraeus', 'flint', 'Volta', 'paterollers', 'Schmalma', 'melanderi', 'bongo', 'hard-to-get', 'Beloved', 'miniscule', 'Tower', 'temerity', 'Fay', 'avidly', ...
Wikipedia:EN	'appropriates', 'Puschmann', 'Muin', 'AC.7', 'sensing', 'Ambas', 'Kalutara', 'Arnott', 'Ogrskem', '48/73', 'Jayan', 'MK2020', 'beauticians', ...
NDA	'disapprove', 'mostly', 'wri+en', '15260', '48104', 'Loving', 'EXCLUSIVE', 'Culver', 'Chih', 'Hwa', 'inch', 'Behalf', 'Opinions', 'HD8', 'appropriated', ...
Purchase Order	'ASNs', 'FRED', 'Party(i)wherethereceivingPartyistheSupplier' 'overturn', 'Navigation', 'work.(iii', 'PLU', 'CDI', 'DFFRUGDQFH', 'INFRINGE', ...
Prime Contracts	'executers', 'Quote', 'derrick', 'FP-1', 'FP-3', 'FP-2', '00:00', 'Ceiling', 'EQUITABLE', 'OBTAIN', 'fan', 'ticket', 'prolonged', 'Macao', '19.2.2(c', ...
Services Agreements	'Sophia(R', 'sacrifice', 'adhesives', 'transloader', 'totheChangeinwriting', 'salient', 'simulate', 'KG', '15/29', 'divert', 'ownedbyCorsearch', 'biologic', ...
Subcontracts	'ENCOURAGED', 'closer', 'INTRODUCTION', 'projecting', '14607', 'CUT', 'Higher', 'interfaces', 'percipient', 'takeover', 'postponement', 'timesheet', ...

paratively infrequently, with a $LF_{C_c,C_b} = -1.43$ Typically, these are anaphoric; the referent is in the exact sentence where the lexical item was used, e.g: "*Employee* agrees that all information communicated to *him/her* concerning the work..." where the referrent is contained in the same sentence as the pronoun. Use of these pronouns are comparatively rare in contracts.

Forms of "they" and "we" appear comparatively infreqently as well, with an $LF_{C_c,C_b} = -0.64$ and $LF_{C_c,C_b} = -0.54$ respectively. Contracts occasionally will use "we" to denote one of the parties involved in the agreement. Similarly, forms of "you" appear quite often compared to other pronouns, with $LF_{C_c,C_b} = -0.12$. In fact, compared against Wikipedia, the $LF_{C_c,\text{Wikipedia}} = 0.57$, which means contracts use "you" far more often than it is found in Wikipedia. "you" simply does not make sense in an encyclopedic style, while on the other hand, contracts will use "you" in a similar manner to "we," defining who exactly "you" refers to at the beginning and never changing throughout, for example, "...the terms "*you and your*" are used in this Agreement, the same shall be construed as including..." defines exactly who "you" refers to. Thus, because "you" always refers to the same entity or set of entities throughout a document and because its deictic quality makes it unambiguous, this allows for its occasional use in contracts.

Last of all, forms of "it" appeared with an $LF_{C_c,C_b} = -0.11$. Like with the rare uses of "he" or "she," "it" is also used in tightly constrained contexts where the referent appears in close proximity to the pronoun it refers to, e.g: "Each *Contract Party* warrants that *it* has the right to make disclosures..." has both the referent and the pronoun in the same sentence, like "he/him" above. Similarly, the cataphoric use remains as well, e.g: "...*it* is *the intention of the Recipient* to give the Information Provider the broadest possible protection..." has the same local quality as the anaphoric use of "it." Nevertheless, forms of "it" appear less often than in the baseline corpora. It is often preferred to using "he," "she," or "they" to refer to one of the defined parties in a contract, though it is still used 23% less often than expected.

As we can see, pronouns such as "she," "he," and "they" appear far less often than in other English corpora; "it" is often used instead, parties are referred to with the pronouns "we" and "you," or the explicit name of the party is used. Even so, these pronouns appear with less frequently than expected. This makes problems like anaphora resolution—one of the more sophisticated components of a coreference resolution system and quite a challenge typically—less difficult to perform on contract language.

5   Nearest Neighbors

Section (4) showed clear differences in the distribution of tokens between contract corpora and the baseline corpora. But tokens alone do not entail repetition, especially if contracts are using the same tokens but in novel ways. One technique to address this question is to compare the sentences within a corpus—to find, for every sentence in the corpus, what the next most similar sentence is. This gives some idea of how repetitive a corpus is at the sentential level.

We considered an information theoretic approach to this problem (Shannon, 1948; Harris, 2002; Crocker et al., 2016; Degaetano-Ortlieb and Teich, 2018). However, we wanted results that were as accessible as possible to a more general audience, and information theoretic results require some initiation in the nuances and meanings of bits and entropy for their meaning to be clear. Instead, we primarily use a unigram vector model (Manning and Schütze, 1999, Section 8.5.1). In a unigram vector model, values derive from an intuitive pairing of identical tokens. Additionally, since the range of possible values falls on a scope from zero to one, their reflection of the similarity between sentences is clear as well, with 0.0 indicating no shared tokens and 1.0 meaning that all tokens between two sentences are shared.

In this section, we conduct a second analysis of the corpora, in this case on a sentence-by-sentence basis, as opposed to merely looking at the rankings individual tokens. Our goal is to see, as we add documents from the each corpus to a collection of sentences under consideration, how the distribution of similarities between sentences changes. This will validate whether contract documents are more repetitive at the sentential level.

5.1 Vector Model

From a sequence of tokens, we define a vector v:

$$\vec{v} = w_0\vec{w}_0 + \ldots + w_i\vec{w}_i + \ldots + w_n\vec{w}_n \quad (1)$$

where w_i is the weight of the vector in dimension $\vec{w}_i$, and n is the vocabulary size in the subcorpus under analysis. Each vector dimension corresponds with a token type in the corresponding sentence. We normalize the weights of each vector dimension such that:

$$w_i = \frac{c_i}{\sqrt{\sum_j c_j^2}} \quad (2)$$

where c_i is the counts of token type i in the sentence under analysis. We compute the cosine similarity between two vectors $\vec{v}$ and $\vec{v'}$ with the dot product:

$$\vec{v} \cdot \vec{v'} = \sum_i w_i \times w_i' \quad (3)$$

which is, due to the weighting, valued between 0 and 1.

From each document, vectors are prepared for each sentence. If a sequence is shorter than 5 tokens, it is removed from consideration. Adding one document at a time, and for each sentence in each subcorpus, we compute the highest dot product value with any other sentence in the corpus, excluding itself. This is done by computing all dot products and storing the highest value.

Because of the sheer number of calculations, this is quite a computationally intensive experiment. We restrict our analysis to the NDA corpus vs Brown and Wikipedia. Because the number of comparisons grows exponentially, we further restrict our analysis to the first 200 randomly selected (without replacement) documents for each corpus.

5.2 Results

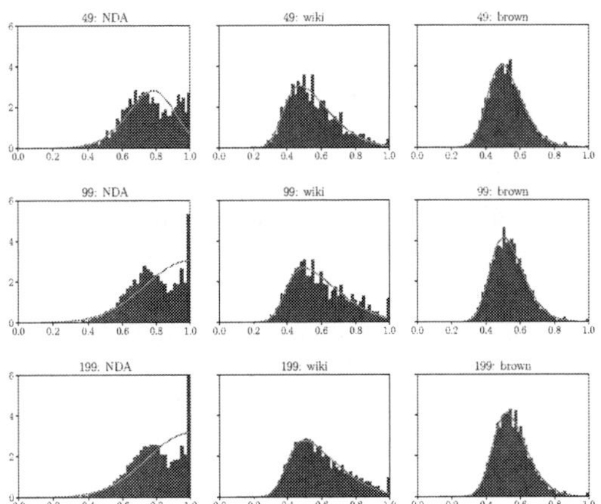

Figure 2: Histograms of the Distribution of Some of the Scores in the Nearest Neighbors Analysis. The histogram bins have a combined area of 1.

After filtering for sequences shorter than 5 tokens, the 200 document subsection of the NDA corpus contains 11,765 sentences; the Brown subsection contains 20,396; the Wikipedia subsection contains 5,385.

Scores generated at some substeps are featured in Figure (2). For the distribution of scores at each step, we fit a skewed normal distribution (Azzalini and Capitanio, 1999), as implemented in SciPy.[7] All fits were statistically significant ($p < 0.001$) past 22 documents. Figure (2) shows histograms

---

[7] https://www.scipy.org/

of the distribution of scores at three samples of these steps at 50, 100, and 200 documents.

Table 4: Statistics of the Distribution of Scores by Number of Docs. "Average" refers to the average of all scores at that point. "Frac Max" refers to the fraction of scores in the highest bin between 0.98 and 1.

Corpus	Statistic	@ 50	@ 100	@ 200
NDA	Average	0.760	0.783	0.791
Wiki	Average	0.551	0.592	0.590
Brown	Average	0.524	0.536	0.552
NDA	Frac Max	4.69%	10.65%	12.15%
Wiki	Frac Max	0.89%	2.03%	1.58%
Brown	Frac Max	0.11%	0.15%	0.26%

Over all, as documents are added, the average scores slowly trend upward (Table 4) between three and four percent. The number of sentences that are near exact matches ("Frac Max") increases dramatically in the NDA corpus compared with the baseline corpora as documents are added, with almost 8% of the scores moving to the near-exact match bin. With respect to the baseline corpora, this barely moved or decreased slightly.

5.3 Discussion

The results indicate quite clearly that repetition is even more salient at the sentential level than at the token level. While we saw trends in the tokens that showed a greater extent of repetition in the contract corpora at large, it is clear this holds at the sentential level, at least for NDAs, with an average sentence similarity that is 20% higher over all. Further, the number of sentences that are identical at 200 documents is almost 11% greater in the NDA data than in the baseline corpora.

Looking closely at the exact matches—sentences with a neighbor from 0.98 to 1.0—many in the NDA corpus are identically worded sentences. However, they are not identical enough that exact string matching is sufficient—for example, they contain the same word types with different capitalization and punctuation. There are, of course, examples of exact repetition in the baseline corpora too. Wikipedia articles contain infoboxes that appear in multiple articles, and parts of them parsed as sentences are exact matches. Brown newswire contains datelines, some of which are the same between articles: e.g. "Miami, Fla., March 17 –". The repetition of exact phrases is not a linguistic phenomenon unique to contracts; however, its frequency is greatly increased.

Most sentences in all corpora do not have an exact match. The average gives us some idea of the kind of match a typical sentence can make. Cosine distance at the sentential level is quite picky. These two pairs of sentences both have the average similarity of around 0.79:

(1a) Any assignment without such written consent shall be null and void and of no force or effect.

(1b) Any such attempted assignment shall be void and of no effect.

(2a) Notwithstanding any other provision of this Agreement to the contrary, this Agreement shall be effective as of the date first above written and shall remain in full force and effect thereafter for a period of two (2) years, whereupon the Agreement shall automatically terminate, unless otherwise terminated by the mutual written agreement of the Parties.

(2b) This Agreement shall be effective as of the Effective Date and continue for a period of five (5) years, or until termination of the Relationship, unless this Agreement is earlier terminated by mutual written agreement of the parties.

We can see clear similarities between the pairs of sentences. Both perform roughly the same function in a contract, albeit with some variation in wording and specific parameters. This shows that even a simple alignment technique can provide quality alignments between similar sentences across contracts, and given that this is the average similarity, that contracts indeed share quite a lot in common with one another, even when that is not an exact match between the two.

Examining the distributions of each of the steps, clearly both the Brown and Wikipedia corpora are modeled quite well by the skew normal distributions, with the curves clearly following the histograms they describe. The skew distribution of the NDA corpus also fits significantly, though the fit does not so obviously model the data; the sheer number of counts contained in the data allowed for the model to be significant. It may be better modeled by a superposition of two distributions, one covering near exact matches and the other covering the broader distribution. Such a model may parametrically work to model the exact matches in the other two baseline corpora too, resulting in improved modeling for those as well.

Regardless of how we judge these models, the degree of repetition in NDAs is much greater than the two baseline corpora, with a great quantity of scores skewed toward 1.0, and even the secondary peak appearing just below 0.8, while the two baseline corpora peak between 0.5 and 0.6. By any measure, the NDA corpus is far more repetitive at the sentential level than its baseline counterparts.

6 Discussion

Contract language, as opposed to most natural language corpora typically studied, is far less variable, exhibiting far fewer rare word types and a much higher sentence similarity. These meet our expectations, and we can definitively state the extent to which contract language is repetitive: hapax legomena appear with $1/5^{th}$ the frequency of other corpora and sentences are 20% more similar on average. These are big differences, but not so big that they defy expectation.

One may be tempted to take this to the extreme and claim that the content of contracts is itself not language at all,[8] but this is a slippery slope fallacy. There is middle ground between newswire and non-language; while contract language may be more repetitive, this does not entail that it is not language. In fact, repetition is a core element of all language. With respect to tokens, this is embodied in the quantitative Zipf's law, but even at the discourse level, notions of repetition like *intertextuality* facilitate what we say and why we say it (Kristeva, 1980). Idioms like "I pronounce you husband and wife" have been uttered millions of times, but that does not remove them from the scope of human language; rather, it endows them with deeper meaning. Beyond a surplus of repetition, the contract corpora exhibit the properties of language; while certain edge cases may be amplified (exact sentence matches) and others reduced (hapax legomena), this is a difference in parameters, not a fundamental difference in form. For

---

[8]A reviewer claimed that we were arguing against a strawman, and that no one would claim that contracts are not language. However, this is an actual claim—albeit one that was not subject to peer-review—made by a company in the legal technology space, "For the purpose of AI training, [technical legal] language cannot be considered a natural language. For contract review and approval, Natural Language Processing (NLP) and off-the-shelf solutions do not work." (https://images.law.com/contrib/content/ uploads/documents/397/5408/lawgeex.pdf)

these reasons, the analysis of contract language remains intrinsically linguistic.

A more formal expression of the source of repetition in contract language is the fact that the speech act (Austin, 1962) performed by a contract itself is repetitive. While newswire and encyclopediae are focused on communicating new information to a reader, contracts are focused on creating arrangements between parties, similar to those created before. This is a very different illocutionary and perlocutionary act. Consequentially, contracts provide a new set of speech acts to study in NLP research, rarely seen in many of the genres of text frequently studied. However, a classification and examination of speech acts in both sets of corpora goes well beyond the scope of this study.

7 Conclusion

In this study, we documented the differences between contract documents and the sort ubiquitous in computational linguistics. Contract documents feature fewer hapax legomena, fewer pronouns, and much higher inter-sentence similarities; however, these similarities are not so redundant that the need for linguistic analysis is mitigated. This demonstrates both the need for new models of language specific to contract language and also the potential reciprocal benefits to research in linguistics and computational linguistics, as contract corpora can reduce the frequency of certain phenomena compared with the sort of corpora typically studied. We also hope in the future to potentially extend this analysis to other legal corpora and case reports.

Acknowledgments

Thanks to Tony Davis. Also, we would like to thank the reviewers, whose interest and feedback has inseparably made this work stronger.

References

Robert Anderson and Jeffrey Manns. 2017. Engineering greater efficiency in mergers and acquisitions. *The Business Lawyer*, 72:657–678.

Patrizia Anesa. 2007. Vagueness and precision in contracts: a close relationship. *Linguistica e filologia*, 24:7–38.

Shlomo Argamon, Paul Chase, and Jeff Dodick. 2005. The languages of science: A corpus-based study of experimental and historical science articles. In *Proceedings of the Annual Meeting of the Cognitive Science Society*, volume 27.

J.L. Austin. 1962. *How To Do Things With Words*. Harvard University Press.

Adelchi Azzalini and Antonella Capitanio. 1999. Statistical applications of the multivariate skew normal distribution. *Journal of the Royal Statistical Society: Series B (Statistical Methodology)*, 61(3):579–602.

S. Bird, E. Loper, and E. Klein. 2009. *Natural Language Processing with Python*. O'Reilly Media Inc.

Bjarne Blom and Anna Trosborg. 1992. An Analysis of Regulative Speech Acts in English Contracts - Qualitative and Quantitative Methods. *Quantitative and quantitative methods. Hermes (Aarhus)*, 82:83.

Daniel P. Broderick, Jonathan Herr, and Daniel E. Simonson. 2016. Method and System for Suggesting Revisions to an Electronic Document. U.S. Patent and Trademark Office, US20170039176A1/US10216715B2.

Luciana Carvalho. 2008. Translating contracts and agreements: a Corpus Linguistics perspective. *Avanços da linguística de Corpus no Brasil*, page 333.

Matthew W. Crocker, Vera Demberg, and Elke Teich. 2016. Information density and linguistic encoding (ideal). *KI - Künstliche Intelligenz*, 30(1):77–81.

Michael Curtotti and Eric C. McCreath. 2011. A Corpus of Australian Contract Language: Description, Profiling and Analysis. In *Proceedings of the 13th International Conference on Artificial Intelligence and Law*, ICAIL '11, pages 199–208, New York, NY, USA. ACM.

Mark Davies. 2010. The Corpus of Contemporary American English as the first reliable monitor corpus of English. *Literary and linguistic computing*, 25(4):447–464.

Stefania Degaetano-Ortlieb and Elke Teich. 2017. Modeling intra-textual variation with entropy and surprisal: topical vs. stylistic patterns. In *Proceedings of the Joint SIGHUM Workshop on Computational Linguistics for Cultural Heritage, Social Sciences, Humanities and Literature*, pages 68–77, Vancouver, Canada. Association for Computational Linguistics.

Stefania Degaetano-Ortlieb and Elke Teich. 2018. Using relative entropy for detection and analysis of periods of diachronic linguistic change. In *Proceedings of the Second Joint SIGHUM Workshop on Computational Linguistics for Cultural Heritage, Social Sciences, Humanities and Literature*, pages 22–33, Santa Fe, New Mexico. Association for Computational Linguistics.

Dorrit Faber and Karen Lauridsen. 1991. The compilation of a Danish-English-French corpus in contract law. *English computer corpora. Selected papers and research guide*, pages 235–43.

W. Nelson Francis and Henry Kučera. 1964, 1971, 1979. *A Standard Corpus of Present-Day Edited American English, for use with Digital Computers (Brown)*. Brown University, Providence, Rhode Island, USA.

Michael AK Halliday. 1988. On the language of physical science. *Registers of Written English: Situational Factors and Linguistic Features*, pages 162–178.

Zellig S Harris. 2002. The structure of science information. *Journal of biomedical informatics*, 35(4):215–221.

Matthew Honnibal and Mark Johnson. 2015. An improved non-monotonic transition system for dependency parsing. In *Proceedings of the 2015 Conference on Empirical Methods in Natural Language Processing*, pages 1373–1378, Lisbon, Portugal. Association for Computational Linguistics.

Jason King. 2018. English Wikipedia Articles 2017-08-20 SQLite. Kaggle.

Julia Kristeva. 1980. *Desire in language: A semiotic approach to literature and art*. Columbia University Press.

Christian Mair. 1997. The spread of the going-to-future in written English: A corpus-based investigation into language change in progress. *Trends in Linguistics Studies and Monographs*, 101:1537–1544.

Christopher D Manning and Hinrich Schütze. 1999. *Foundations of Statistical Natural Language Processing*. MIT Press.

Abdel Karim Mohammad, Nabil Alawi, and Maram Fakhouri. 2010. Translating contracts between english and arabic: Towards a more pragmatic outcome. *Jordan Journal of Modern Languages and Literature*.

Jane Norre Nielsen and Anne Wichmann. 1994. A frequency analysis of selected modal expressions in German and English legal texts. *HERMES-Journal of Language and Communication in Business*, 7(13):145–155.

Claude Elwood Shannon. 1948. A mathematical theory of communication. *Bell system technical journal*, 27(3):379–423.

George K. Zipf. 1949. *Human Behavior and the Principle of Least Effort*. Addison-Wesley.

Sentence Boundary Detection in Legal Text

George Sanchez
Thomson Reuters R&D
610 Opperman Dr. Eagan, MN 55123
`FName.LName@TR.com`

Abstract

In this paper, we examined several algorithms to detect sentence boundaries in legal text. Legal text presents challenges for sentence tokenizers because of the variety of punctuations, linguistic structure, and syntax of legal text. Out-of-the-box algorithms perform poorly on legal text affecting further analysis of the text. A novel and domain-specific approach is needed to detect sentence boundaries to further analyze legal text. We present the results of our investigation in this paper.

1 Introduction

Sentence Boundary Detection (SBD) is an important fundamental task in any Natural Language Processing (NLP) application because errors tend to propagate to high-level tasks and because the obviousness of SBD errors can lead users to question the correctness and value of an entire product. While SBD is regarded as a solved problem in many domains, legal text presents unique challenges. The remainder of this paper describes those challenges and evaluates three approaches to the task, including a modification to a commonly-used semi-supervised and rule-based library as well as two supervised sequence labeling approaches. We find that a fully-supervised approach is superior to the semi-supervised rule library.

2 Previous Work

There are several out-of-the-box algorithms for SBD. Most of these algorithms are available in the most commonly used natural language processing (NLP) libraries. These algorithms for SBD are a product of years of research and study of natural language processing. SBD has not recently received much attention from the NLP community (Read, 2012) and is almost always considered a side issue in most NLP research efforts (Walker, 2001). Most of the algorithms like decision tree classifier (Riley, 1989), Naïve Bayes and Support Vector Machine (SVM) based models as reviewed in (Gillick, 2009), and the Punkt unsupervised model (Kiss, 2006) proved to be highly accurate and adequate for most domain language data, such as collections of news articles. These algorithms common in NLP toolkits often perform rather poorly in specific domains like the biomedical domain (Griffis, 2016). We observe the same poor performance on legal and tax documents when an untrained unmodified PunktSentenceTokenizer in NLTK (Bird, 2009) was used in Section 5. Algorithms such as Punkt, need to be customized and trained for a specific domain to be effective.

3 Experiments

We reviewed the following approach:

- Punkt Model with Custom Abbreviations

- Conditional Random Field

- Deep Learning Neural Networks

In-house rule-based SBD gathered from subject matter experts in the organization, where the author is employed at, is reaching its limits when used to process newer legal documents because more current legal documents have complex structures. Python's Natural Language Toolkit (NLTK) Punkt model proved to be good enough for some time that we were able to develop several customized models. This unsupervised model approach with Punkt allowed us greater flexibility to adapt to several collections of legal and tax documents.

Proceedings of the Natural Legal Language Processing Workshop 2019, pages 31–38
Minneapolis, Minesotta, June 7, 2019. ©2019 Association for Computational Linguistics

Nonetheless, we still found some situations that the customized Punkt models were not able to handle. So, we started looking into other methods for SBD. In this paper, we compare Punkt, our customized Punkt model, a Conditional Random Field (CRF) model, and a deep learning neural network approach. Our investigation used the publicly available data in (Savelka, 2017), available at `https://github.com/jsavelka/sbd_adju` `dicatory_dec/tree/master/data_set`

4   SBD Challenges in Legal Text

Legal texts are more challenging for SDB than most domain language data like news articles because most legal texts are structured into sections and subsections, not like the narrative structure of a news article. Legal texts contain some or all of the following elements header, footer, footnotes, or lists. The most important sections or discussion in legal text are interleaved with citations. The sentences may be extended or spread across lists.

Legal texts also have a very particular linguistic structure. These are spans of text that doesn't follow a standard sentence structure but is considered important part of the text. Here are some problematic language structures that affect SBD in legal text (Savelka, 2017):

- **Case names in document** titles are best treated as a sentence legal text. e.g., *UNITED STATES of America, Plaintiff–Appellee, v. Matthew R. LANGE, Defendant–Appellant.*

- **Headings** in legal text provides information about the organization of the text. The headings chunk the text into meaningful segments or issues. e.g., ARGUMENT

  INTRODUCTION

  I. BACKGROUND

- **Fields** with values that provide the name of the field e.g.,

  DOCKET NO. A–4462–13T2

  Prison Number: #176948

- **Page Numbers** that refers to reporter service prints containing cited or discussed text e.g., *59 During a search of the defendant's closed, but unlocked

  *1163 See United States v. Pina-Jaime, 332 F.3d 609, 612 (9th Cir.2003)

- **Ellipses** in sentences indicate missing words or indicate that some sentences have been deleted. This is often used for quoted text. e.g., *...After granting discretionary review, the Supreme Court, Aker, J., held that rule, which stated that court*

- **Parentheticals** within sentences often occur with citations. e.g., see also United States v. Infante-Ruiz, *13 F.3d 498, 504-505 (1st Cir.1994)* (when third party consent to search vehicle and trunk is qualified by a warning that the briefcase belonged to another, officers could not assume without further inquiry that the consent extended to the briefcase)

- **Enumerated lists** (whether numbered or lettered) e.g.,

  FINDINGS OF FACT

  1. The Veteran does meet the criteria for a diagnosis of posttraumatic stress disorder (PTSD).

- **Endnotes or footnotes** text indicator often occur near sentence boundaries. e.g., *and three counts of possession of device-making equipment, 18 U.S.C. § 1029(a)(4).[2]*

- **Citations in sentences** e.g., Thus, even an "infinitesimal contribution to the disability might require full contribution." *(Id., at pp. 430–431, 133 Cal.Rptr. 809.)* The Heaton court also rejected this argument, noting that section 31722 explicitly provided for mental as well as physical disabilities.

The dataset used for the experiments in this paper were carefully annotated to address how each of the described situations above was treated. Protocols were put in place to have consistency as to what is considered a "sentence" in the dataset.

Please see (Savelka, 2017) for a thorough discussion of how the sentences in the dataset were annotated.

5 Data

The dataset contains decisions in the United States Courts (Savelka, 2017). The dataset is in four files bva.json, cyber_crime.json, intellectual_property.json, and scotus.json. All of the experiments used the bva.json, intellectual_property.json, and scotus.json for training and development of the model. Each model was tested on cyber_crime.json. Each file contains several decisions with the full text of the decision and a list of offsets of sentence boundaries in the text. The sentences were extracted using the offsets provided to prepare the data for training. Each sentence was tokenized to create breaks between numbers, alphabetic characters, and punctuation. Then, each token was labeled 'B' – Beginning 'I' -Inside, 'L'–Last. Example:

Sentence:
```
See United States v. Bailey, 227
F.3d 792, 797 (7th Cir.2000);
```
Tokens:
```
['See', 'United', 'States', 'v',
'.', 'Bailey', ',', '227', 'F', '.
', '3', 'd', '792', ',', '797', '
(', '7', 'th', 'Cir', '.', '2000',
')', ';']
```
Label:
```
['B', 'I', 'I', 'I', 'I', 'I', 'I
', 'I', 'I', 'I', 'I', 'I', 'I', '
I', 'I', 'I', 'I', 'I', 'I', 'I',
'I', 'I', 'L']
```

After pre-processing all the Adjudicat ory decisions, the dataset contains 80 documents, 26052 sentences, and the following distribution of labels.

```
{'B': 25126,'I': 658870, 'L': 26052}
```

6 Punkt Experiment

The Punkt model is an unsupervised algorithm with an assumption that SBD can be improved if abbreviations are correctly detected and then eliminated (Kiss, 2006). In our investigation of Punkt, we used the PunktSentenceTokenizer without further training and a trained instance with modified abbreviations.

6.1 Punkt (unmodified/untrained) Results

Predicted	Actual		
	B	I	L
B	6652	1019	103
I	3121	188114	3525
L	136	1298	6861

Table 1– Punkt(untrained/unmodified) Confusion Matrix

	Precision	Recall	F1-Score	Support
B	0.671	0.856	0.752	7774
I	0.988	0.966	0.977	194760
L	0.654	0.827	0.731	8295
Weighted Avg	0.963	0.956	0.959	210829
Weighted Avg Excluding 'I'	0.662	0.841	0.741	16069

Table 2 – Punkt (untrained/unmodified) Results Report

Table 2 gives us a summary of the results for Precision, Recall, F1-score, and Support of the experiment. The support column is the number of elements in each class label. The majority of labeled tokens are "I" (Inside), but the end of sentence labels "L" (Last), which we need to target, are most important because it is the token label that represents the end of sentences. The unmodified and untrained PunktSentenceTokenizer gave us a weighted average F1-Score of 0.959 (Table 2) including the predictions for tokens "I" (Inside) the sentences. Excluding "I" (Inside), we get a weighted average F1-Score of only 0.741. A precision of around 65.4% (precision for "L" (Last) on Table 2) detecting end of sentences might not be adequate when processing large volumes of legal text. In comparison, (Kiss, 2006) reports an error rate of 1.02% (98.98% Precision) [2] on the Brown corpus and 1.65% (98.35% Precision) on the WSJ. To improve the score of the Punkt model, we trained it and gave it an updated abbreviation list based on the legal text domain. Please see (Appendix A 1) for a sample list of abbreviations that we included in the model.

Additionally, we replace '\n'(newline) and '\t' (tab) with space and "(double quotes) with " (two single quotes) for each sentence used for training. The model was trained to learn parameters unsupervised using the cleaned sentences of training set files. To test the Punkt model, we used the test set file. The test labels

---

2 Precision calculated as 100 − error rate

were generated using the B, I, and L labels as described in (Section 4). Each document in the test set was sentence tokenized using the model then assigned the appropriate B, I, and L labels to generate the predicted labels for the test file.

6.2   Punkt (trained/updated) Results

Predicted	Actual		
	B	I	L
B	6640	1031	103
I	2258	189844	2658
L	135	1311	6849

Table 3 – Punkt (trained/updated) Results Confusion Matrix

	Precision	Recall	F1-Score	Support
B	0.735	0.854	0.790	7774
I	0.988	0.975	0.981	194760
L	0.713	0.826	0.765	8295
Weighted Avg	0.968	0.964	0.966	210829
Weighted Avg Excluding 'I'	0.724	0.839	0.777	16069

Table 4 – Punkt (trained/updated) Results Report

For Punkt, the added abbreviation makes the model slightly better than without training and adding the abbreviation. For the trained and updated model, we get a weighted average F1-Score of 0.966 including the "I" (Inside) labels and 0.777 excluding the "I" (Inside). We see about the same F1-score on the weighted average excluding the "I" (Inside) labels. The precision on "L" (Last) labels slightly increased as well. Precision is still low compared to the performance of Punkt against the Brown corpus and WSJ (Kiss, 2006).

6.3   Punkt SBD Errors

Both   Punkt(untrained/unmodified)   and Punkt(trained/updated) used periods to segment sentences which do not work well with legal text.

```
Sentence segmentation as labeled:
```

```
In Re Application for Pen Register
and Trap/Trace, 396 F. Supp. 2d 74
7 (S.D. Tex. 2005)
District Court, S.D. Texas
Filed: October 14th, 2005
```

```
Punkt segmentation (untrained/unmo
dified and trained/updated):
```

```
In Re Application for Pen Register
and Trap/Trace, 396 F. Supp.
2d 747 (S.D.
Tex.
2005) District Court, S.D.
Texas Filed: October 14th, 2005
```

7   Conditional Random Field Experiment

After Punkt, we evaluate the use of Conditional Random Field (CRF) for SBD. A CRF is a random field conditioned on an observation sequence (Liu, 2005). A sentence is an excellent example of an observation sequence. CRF's are being used successfully for a variety of text processing tasks (Liu, 2005). We build on Savelka's (2017) work on using CRF for SDB for legal text.

7.1   Feature Extraction for CRF Experiment

Features were extracted for each token using a window of 3 tokens before and after the token that is in focus. For those 3 tokens before and after, we extracted a total of 8 features based on the characters in the token. The combination of those features represents a token in our feature space before being used to train the model. The features used in this experiment are based on the simple features mentioned in (Savelka, 2017). Some sample features are IsLower, IsUpper, IsSpace (see Appendix A 2 for feature sample). Using sklearn_crfsuite CRF, the model was trained using a gradient descent L-BFGS method with a maximum of 100 iterations with L1 (0.1) and L2 (0.1) regularization.

7.2   CRF Results

Predicted	Actual		
	B	I	L
B	6738	964	72
I	469	193810	481
L	95	1072	7128

Table 5 - CRF Results Confusion Matrix

	Precision	Recall	F1-Score	Support
B	0.923	0.867	0.894	7774
I	0.990	0.995	0.992	194760
L	0.928	0.859	0.892	8295
Weighted Avg	0.985	0.985	0.985	210829
Weighted Avg Excluding 'I'	0.925	0.863	0.893	16069

Table 6 - CRF Results Report

The CRF model gave us a weighted average F1-Score of 0.985 (Table 6) including the predictions for tokens "I" (Inside) the sentences. Excluding this, we get 0.893. The precision on "L" (Last) labels for the CRF model is acceptable at 92.8%.

As indicated in the frequency distribution (Section 4), the "I" (Inside) labels are the majority of the tokens. The huge number of "I" (Inside) presents an imbalance for this classification task but excluding "I" (Inside) for learning, we would lose the tendencies of the corpus. Keeping the "I" (Inside) during training would preserve the semantics of the sentences.

7.3 CRF SBD Errors

Here are some of the CRF's most common errors:

1. Citations as sentences

Sentence segmentation as labeled:

```
Franklin also moved to dismiss
eleven of the fourteen copyright
infringement counts on the ground
that Apple failed to comply with the
procedural requirements for suit
under
17 U. S. C. § § 410, 411.
< 714 F. 2 d 1245 >
```

CRF's segmentation:

```
Franklin also moved to dismiss ele
ven of the fourteen copyright infr
ingement counts on the ground that
Apple failed to comply with the pr
ocedural requirements for suit und
er 17 U. S. C. § § 410, 411.
< 714 F. 2 d 1245 >
```

2. Semi-colon or colon as a sentence ending.

Sentence segmentation as labeled:

```
Defendants Simon Blitz and Danie
l Gazal are the sole shareholder
s of defendants Cel - Net Commun
ications, Inc. (" Cel - Net ");
The Cellular Network Communicati
ons, Inc., doing business as CNC
G ("CNCG"); and SD Telecommunica
tions, Inc. ("SD Telecom").
```

CRF's segmentation:

```
Defendants Simon Blitz and Daniel
Gazal are the sole shareholders of
defendants Cel - Net Communication
s, Inc. (" Cel - Net"); The Cellul
ar Network Communications, Inc., d
oing business as CNCG ("CNCG"); an
d SD Telecommunications, Inc. (" S
D Telecom ").
```

8   Neural Networks Experiment

After CRF, token context gives a significant performance gain for detecting sentence boundaries. The imbalance of the class labels is an inherent characteristic of the SBD task because sentence endings would occur at a rate, we see in the distribution frequency in written legal text for however many labeled training examples.

We experimented with a deep learning neural network representing sentence tokens as a fixed dimensional vector that encoded the context of the text using word embeddings. Gensim word2vec (Mikolov 2013) was trained on all the Adjudicatory decision data pre-processed as tokens as described in Section 4 in 200 epochs. We used an embedding size of 300 using the skip-gram model with negative sampling. Please see Appendix A 3 for the Gensim Word2vec parameters that were used.

8.1   Neural Network Training

The neural network was trained using the training data, pre-processed as described in Section 4. Each sentence token is represented as the concatenation of the vectors of word2vec embedding using a 3-word window plus 8 features (See Appendix A 4) similar to the one we used in CRF experiment, which will be the input vectors to the network.

The neural network model's architecture is a stack of Bi-Directional LSTM with a softmax output layer.

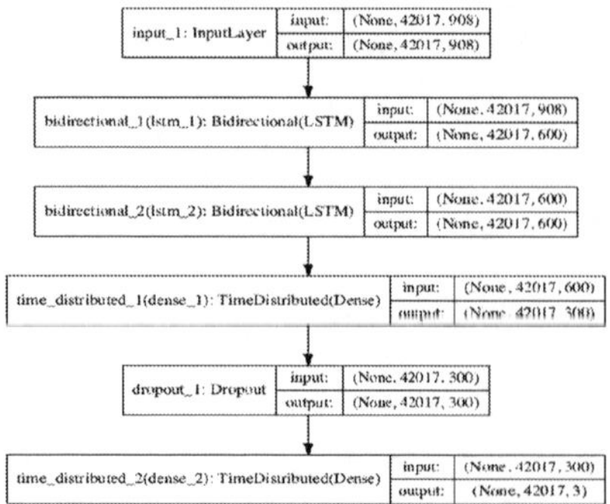

Figure 1- Neural Network Architecture

The model was trained for 40 epochs using an Adam optimizer with learning rate set to 0.001 and categorical cross-entropy as the loss function, a validation split of 15% and shuffling. We opted to use categorical cross-entropy because of its tendency to perform well on an imbalanced training set. Early stopping was also employed for up to 38 out of the 40 epochs (model training will stop if we see the model's loss increase after 38 epochs). The model was tested using the test data set.

8.2 Neural Network Results

Predicted	Actual		
	B	I	L
B	6993	668	113
I	816	193158	786
L	95	870	7330

Table 7 - Neural Network Results Confusion Matrix

	Precision	Recall	F1-Score	Support
B	0.885	0.900	0.892	7774
I	0.992	0.992	0.992	194760
L	0.891	0.884	0.887	8295
Weighted Avg	0.984	0.984	0.984	210829
Weighted Avg Excluding 'I'	0.888	0.891	0.890	16069

Table 8 - Neural Network Results Report

8.3 Neural Network SBD Errors

1. Periods took on a different context.
   Sentence segmentation as labeled:
   TRW Inc. v. Andrews, 534 U. S. 19 (2001)

Supreme Court of the United States
Filed: November 13th, 2001
Precedential Status: Precedential

NN's Segmentation:
TRW Inc. v.
Andrews, 534 U. S. 19 (2001) Supreme Court of the United States Filed: November 13th, 2001 Precedential

Sentence segmentation as labeled:
See 15 U. S. C. § § 1681 n, 1681 o (1994 ed.). [2]
The facts of this case are for the most part undisputed.

NN's Segmentation:
.) . [2] The facts of this case are for the most part undisputed.

2. Specific tokens as sentence endings, e.g., "the," "With."

Sentence segmentation as labeled:
With him on the briefs was Harold R. Fatzer, Attorney General.
John W. Davis argued the cause for appellees in No. 2 on the original argument and for appellees in Nos. 2 and 4 on the reargument.
H. Albert Young, Attorney General of Delaware, argued the cause for petitioners in No. 10 on the original argument and on the reargument.
With him on the briefs was Louis J. Finger, Special Deputy Attorney General.

NN's segmentation:
With
him on the briefs was Harold R. Fatzer, Attorney General. John W. Davis argued the cause for appellees in No. 2 on the original argument and for appellees in Nos. 2 and 4 on the reargument. H. Albert Young, Attorne

```
y General of Delaware, argu
ed the
cause for petitioners in N
o. 10 on the original argum
ent and on the reargument.
With him on the briefs was
Louis J. Finger, Special De
puty
```

9   Conclusion

Out of the box sentence tokenization from popular NLP libraries like NLTK maybe be good enough for most general domain NLP tasks. However, in the legal domain, a Punkt model needs to be trained and updated to have reasonable performance on SBD especially for use with large bodies of legal text. The custom abbreviations with the Punkt model that we use are a product of the legal expertise within our organization. Without such expertise, labeled legal domain text can be used to train several algorithms to do SBD on legal text.

The CRF approach proves to be the most practical approach after comparing the results of our experiment. The neural network model's performance on token classification did not translate to a better SBD compared to the CRF Model. Ease of training and testing are an advantage of using the CRF approach. There is room for future improvement for both the CRF and the neural network approaches. For CRF, collocation features might be helpful. A different word embedding like BERT or weight balancing might improve the performance for the deep learning neural network model.

The publicly available data used in the experiments above are limited and constrained, but it is a good starting point. There is a lot more variety of legal text that was not represented in the data — for example, tax documents, dockets, and headnotes.

References

Read, J., Dridan, R., Oepen, S., & Solberg, L. J. (2012). *Sentence boundary detection: A long solved problem?.* Proceedings of COLING 2012: Posters, 985-994.

Walker, D. J., Clements, D. E., Darwin, M., & Amtrup, J. W. (2001, September). *Sentence boundary detection: A comparison of paradigms for improving MT quality.* In Proceedings of the MT Summit VIII (Vol. 58).

Riley MD. *Some applications of tree-based modeling to speech and language.* Proc Work Speech Nat Lang. 1989;(2):339–52.

Gillick, D. (2009). *Sentence boundary detection and the problem with the US. In Proceedings of Human Language Technologies*: The 2009 Annual Conference of the North American Chapter of the Association for Computational Linguistics, Companion Volume: Short Papers (pp. 241-244).

Kiss, T., & Strunk, J. (2006). *Unsupervised multilingual sentence boundary detection.* Computational Linguistics, 32(4), 485-525.

Bird, S., Klein, E., & Loper, E. (2009). *Natural language processing with Python: analyzing text with the natural language toolkit.* " O'Reilly Media, Inc.".

Griffis, D., Shivade, C., Fosler-Lussier, E., & Lai, A. M. (2016). *A quantitative and qualitative evaluation of sentence boundary detection for the clinical domain.* AMIA Summits on Translational Science Proceedings, 2016, 88.

Liu, Y., Stolcke, A., Shriberg, E., & Harper, M. (2005). *Using conditional random fields for sentence boundary detection in speech.* In Proceedings of the 43rd Annual Meeting of the Association for Computational Linguistics (ACL'05) (pp. 451-458).

Savelka, J., Walker, V. R., Grabmair, M., & Ashley, K. D. (2017). *Sentence boundary detection in adjudicatory decisions in the united states.* Traitement Automatique des langues, 58(2), 21-45.

Palmer, D. D., & Hearst, M. A. (1997). *Adaptive multilingual sentence boundary disambiguation.* Computational Linguistics, 23(2), 241-267.

Mikolov, T., Sutskever, I., Chen, K., Corrado, G. S., & Dean, J. (2013). *Distributed representations of words and phrases and their compositionality.* Advances in neural information processing systems, 3111-3119.

A   Appendices

1.   Custom Abbreviation List

```
['sec','jan','feb','mar','apr','m
ay','jun','jul','aug','sep','sept
','oct','nov','dec','b.f','k.o','
l.b','h.e','h.r','o.j','n.j','u.n
','s.b','p.a','s.f','h.b','e.o','
w.s',
'g.i','p.s','g.m','p.c','m.e','a.
w','m.d','m.a','b.s','j.d','b.a',
'i.q','e.r']
```

2. CRF Sample Feature

['bias','0:lower=,','0:sig=,','0:len
gth=1','0:islower=false','0:isupper=
false','0:istitle=false','0:isdigit=
false','0:isspace=false','-3:BOS','-
2:lower=patrick','-2:sig=CCCCCCC','-
2:length=long','-2:islower=false','-
2:isupper=true','-
2:istitle=false','-
2:isdigit=false','-
2:isspace=false','-
1:lower=maloney','-1:sig=CCCCCCC','-
1:length=long','-1:islower=false','-
1:isupper=true','-
1:istitle=false','-
1:isdigit=false','-
1:isspace=false','1:lower=on','1:sig
=cc','1:length=2','1:islower=true','
1:isupper=false','1:istitle=false','
1:isdigit=false','1:isspace=false','
2:lower=behalf','2:sig=cccccc','2:le
ngth=normal','2:islower=true','2:isu
pper=false','2:istitle=false','2:isd
igit=false','2:isspace=false','3:low
er=of','3:sig=cc','3:length=2','3:is
lower=true','3:isupper=false','3:ist
itle=false','3:isdigit=false','3:iss
pace=false']
Legend:
  -3 = before
  -2 = before
  -2 = before
  0 = current token
  1 = after
  2 = after
  3 = after
  bias = string constant
  BOS = Beginning of Sentence
  EOS = End of Sentence
  lower= token in lowercase
  sig= word shape of token
    C=upper case character
    c=lower case character
    D=digit
  length= length of token
    (< 4)= str(len(token))
    (>=4 token <=6) = "normal"
    (>6) = "long"
  islower = binary feature which is
set to true if all token characters
are in lower case
  isupper = binary feature which is
set to true if all token characters
are in upper case
  istitle = binary feature which is
set to true if the first token

character is upper case the rest is
lower case
  isdigit = binary feature which is
set to true if all character tokens
are digits
  isspace = binary feature which is
set to true if all token characters
are whitespace

3. Gensim Word2Vec training parameters

sg=1, hs=1, window=5, min_count=100,
workers=4, negative=10, ns_exponent=1

sg = skip-gram model
hs = use hierarchical softmax
min_count = ignores all words with
total frequency less than this
workers = no. of worker threads
negative = negative sampling
ns_exponent = negative sampling
distribution value of 1.0 samples are
proportional to the frequencies

4. Neural Network input additional Features

isUpper = binary feature which is set
to true if all token characters are
in upper case
  isLower= binary feature which is set
to true if all token characters are
in lower case
  isDigit= binary feature which is set
to true if all character tokens are
digits
  isSpace= binary feature which is set
to true if all token characters are
whitespace
  isPunctuation= binary feature which
is set to true if the token is a
punctuation
  Next Word Capitalized = binary
feature which is set to true if the
next word's first character is
capitalized
  Previous Word Lower= binary feature
which is set to true if the previous
word's first character is in lower
case
  Previous Word Single Char= binary
feature which is set to true if the
previous word a single character

Legal Linking: Citation Resolution and Suggestion in Constitutional Law

Robert Shaffer[*]
Perry World House
University of Pennsylvania
shafferr@upenn.edu

Stephen Mayhew[*]
Computer and Information Science
University of Pennsylvania
mayhew@seas.upenn.edu

Abstract

This paper describes a dataset and baseline systems for linking paragraphs from court cases to clauses or amendments in the US Constitution. We implement a rule-based system, a linear model, and a neural architecture for matching pairs of paragraphs, taking training data from online databases in a distantly-supervised fashion. In experiments on a manually-annotated evaluation set, we find that our proposed neural system outperforms a rules-driven baseline. Qualitatively, this performance gap seems largest for abstract or indirect links between documents, which suggests that our system might be useful for answering political science and legal research questions or discovering novel links. We release the dataset along with the manually-annotated evaluation set to foster future work.

1 Introduction

Authors of legal texts are frequently interested in understanding how their document relates to a knowledge base or to some reference text or corpus. Because legal reasoning relies on references to preexisting precedent, identifying the documents or document sections (e.g. court cases; constitutional provisions) that relate to the author's current argument or topic of interest is an important task. However, constructing these reference links is labor-intensive, particularly if the set of reference texts is large or the link is ambiguous. Automating this linkage task therefore offers useful assistance for authors of legal texts.

Linking systems of this kind are also useful for answering important political science and legal research questions. For example, in US Constitutional law, the Supreme Court has anecdotally appeared more receptive to arguments that combine multiple Constitutional rights.[1] However, without an automated linking system, identifying instances of rhetorical "commingling" of rights is labor-intensive. Outside the American context, even simple data on the frequency with which judges invoke particular constitutional rights are difficult to gather. A generic, automated system capable of inferring links between sections of judicial opinions and related legal texts[2] would therefore be valuable for legal and political science researchers.

With this motivation, we present a method for linking pairs of documents – here, Supreme Court case paragraphs and Constitution sections – based on distantly-annotated training data. Our model operates on the level of short pieces of text, such as paragraphs, and gives a binary decision between pairs of texts, marking a presence or absence of a link. As we describe, a key challenge we face is that our training data are generated using rules-based heuristics, and are thus highly incomplete. As a result, one of our main contributions is a data preprocessing step that "strips" rules-based language from the training data. In our experiments, we find that this step combined with a modern neural network model allows our system to substantially outperform both rules-driven and non-neural baselines on a manually-tagged evaluation set. Qualitatively, this performance gap appears largest for paragraphs that contain abstract or indirect references to Constitutional provisions, which suggests that the system we propose might also be useful for discovering new links not identified by existing techniques.

---

[*]Authors contributed equally. Order chosen by coin flip.

[1]E.g., *Lamb's Chapel v. Center Moriches Union Free School District* (508 U.S. 384) and related religious speech cases, which successfully combine free speech and free exercise of religion arguments. See McCloskey and Levinson (2016, 162-163) for further discussion.

[2]E.g. other national constitutions, as in Elkins et al. (2014).

Proceedings of the Natural Legal Language Processing Workshop 2019, pages 39–44
Minneapolis, Minesotta, June 7, 2019. ©2019 Association for Computational Linguistics

2   Related Work

In the legal domain, initiatives including the Cornell Legal Information Institute have constructed standardized citation templates to assist users interested in linking citations of various formats (see Casanovas et al. (2016) for an overview). However, these systems are not designed to infer ci tations based on plain-text excerpts, which is our problem of interest. Schwartz et al. (2015) propose a topic model-based approach that suggests citations to relevant US Supreme Court case law based on user-inputted free text. Because this system only draws links between excerpts and full Supreme Court cases, it is coarser than ours, but provides perhaps the closest point of comparison in the legal domain (Branting, 2017). A closer comparison point is Nomoto (2018), who propose an approach that infers paragraph-level citation links between published scientific papers.

The methods that we adopt to solve this problem draw inspiration from several fields in natural language processing (NLP) and machine learning, including multilabel classification (Boutell et al., 2004; Nam et al., 2014), dataless classification (Chang et al., 2008), citation resolution (Duma and Klein, 2014), and entity linking (Ratinov et al., 2011; Shen et al., 2015). Our method of collecting training data is reminiscent of distant supervision techniques (Mintz et al., 2009).

3   Data Collection

To obtain training data, we draw on the Cornell Legal Information Institute (Cornell LII)'s repository of US Supreme Court opinion texts.[3] We began by scraping all text associated with all opinions available through the Cornell LII site. For each case, we then removed all HTML markup, editorial information, and other non-opinion language (e.g. footnotes, case summaries, or front matter), and split the remaining text into paragraphs. For each paragraph, we then checked whether that paragraph contained a hyperlink to a section of the US Constitution. If any hyperlinks were present, we stored the paragraph and linked Constitution section(s) as training pair(s). Finally, we removed any duplicate paragraphs. This process left us with a total dataset of $\sim$ 328k unique paragraphs, of which $\sim$ 8k contained at least one link, and a total of $\sim$ 11k links.

Inspecting these data, we noticed that the annotation was inconsistent and incomplete. For example, not all paragraphs with the phrase "First Amendment" linked to the First Amendment. To solve this problem, we manually created a small list of rules for annotation. The list contained about 100 rules, and consisted mainly of mapping amendment names ("Seventh Amendment" or "7th Amendment") to the correct label. We also included several representative phrases, such as "free speech", "due process clause", and others. After this annotation, we had $\sim$ 36k paragraphs with at least one link, and $\sim$ 41k links total.

Though convenient, this process created certain trivial dependencies between linked paragraphs, which might limit a model's ability to generalize. Because hyperlinks and rules are associated with text, all linked paragraphs necessarily contain rule strings that correspond to the linked Constitution section. For example, all paragraphs that link to the First Amendment necessarily contain rule strings such as "First Amendment", "1st Amendment", or "Amendment I". A model trained on this dataset would likely treat the presence/absence of strings like these as strong classification signals, which is undesirable if the goal is to identify links between paragraphs that do not explicitly mention the name of the linked paragraph.

To encourage the model to move beyond these trivial patterns, we therefore create a modified copy of our training set, which we term the "stripped" dataset. In the "stripped" dataset, we randomly select half of the training examples, and delete all hyperlink or rule strings that occur within the text of these training examples, leaving potentially disfluent sentences. We delete hyperlink and rule strings from only half of training examples because presence of a phrase such as "First Amendment" is still a strong linking signal which we would like to preserve.

In our evaluations, we assess model performance on both the original and "stripped" datasets separately. We emphasize that this "stripping" process does *not* change the number of observations in either our training or evaluation sets. Instead, the "stripping" step simply removes rule strings from certain training examples, which (we suggest) compels our downstream tagging model to move beyond simply re-learning the rules we use to construct our training set.

---

[3] https://www.law.cornell.edu/

3.1 Manual Annotations

To assess model performance, we hand-annotated Constitutional references in all paragraphs ($n = 1241$) from an additional five Supreme Court cases: *Griswold v. Connecticut* (381 U.S. 479), *Miranda v. Arizona* (384 U.S. 436), *US v. Nixon* (418 U.S. 683), *Texas v. Johnson* (491 U.S. 397), and *NFIB v. Sebelius* (567 U.S. 519). We emphasize that these cases were *not* selected randomly. Since most Supreme Court cases infrequently reference the Constitution, we chose these cases because they litigate important constitutional law questions, and are therefore likely to contain a high density of positive examples with which to assess model performance.

These five cases provide two other desirable properties for an evaluation set. First, each of these cases addresses a different legal issue (e.g. criminal rights in *Miranda*; free speech in *Texas v. Johnson*). As a result, each case is likely to contain references to a distinct set of Constitutional provisions. Second, these cases also vary substantially in rhetorical style. For example, Justice Douglas's opinion in *Griswold* famously references and connects the "penumbras" of various Constitutional provisions in order to identify a right to privacy. Since most of these references consist of passing references to standard provision names (e.g. "First Amendment"; "Due Process Clause"), we expect the links in *Griswold* to be "easy" to predict. By contrast, *US v. Nixon* and *NFIB v. Sebelius* tackle abstract questions regarding the scope of Presidential and Congressional powers. As a result, they are more likely to indirectly reference Constitutional provisions, thus providing a more substantial challenge, and more room to improve.

4 Methods

Our data are defined in terms of input documents D, and reference documents C. The goal of the task is to link an input document $d \in D$ to zero or more reference documents. Formally, we will create a model of the form $h(d) \rightarrow \mathbf{y}$, where $\mathbf{y} \in \{0,1\}^{|C|}$ and $\mathbf{y}_i = 1$ if d is to be linked to document $c_i \in C$. If $\mathbf{y} = \{0\}^{|C|}$, this means that d links to no paragraph (true for most pieces of text, including this paragraph).

We emphasize that our aim in this preliminary work is not to discover the best architecture for this task, but to provide strong baselines for future work to build on.

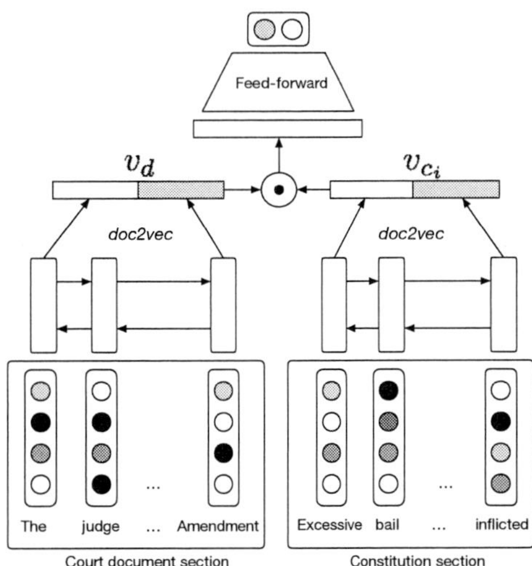

Figure 1: Diagram of the neural network architecture for a single binary classifier in the multilabel space. Token embeddings are from BERT, and we use a single *doc2vec* for both paragraphs. This system is described in Section 4.3, and corresponds to equations (1)-(3). The $\odot$ refers to element-wise multiplication.

4.1 Rule-based

An intuitive baseline is to use the rules defined for the annotation process as the entire labeling strategy. Instead of applying these rules to the training data, we apply them to the test data directly. As with any rule-based system, we would expect that this achieves high precision and low recall.

4.2 Linear Model

Beyond the rule-based system, we also implemented a linear multi-label classifier. Our implementation is a variant of the so-called Binary Relevance framework (Boutell et al., 2004; Nam et al., 2014), which builds a separate classifier for each label. As such, the problem decomposes to building C separate classifiers: $h(d) \rightarrow \{h_i(d)\}_{i=1}^{|C|}$, where $h_i(d) \rightarrow \{0,1\}$.

We used logistic regression as the model, and used unigrams, bigrams, and trigrams as features. Since the training data is wildly imbalanced towards unmatched paragraphs, we employ two tricks in our training. First, as a preprocessing step, we selected all examples with links, but subsampled the unmatched examples such that there was an equal number of matched and unmatched. Second, we downweighted all negative examples in training by a constant factor. This deals with the fact that every positive example for one class

Model	P	R	F1
Rule-based	**91.8**	47.0	62.2
Linear (original)	79.0	45.8	58.0
Linear (stripped)	68.3	54.3	60.5
Neural Network (original)	82.1	46.8	59.6
Neural Network (stripped)	76.5	**56.2**	**64.8**

Table 1: Results on the manually annotated test set. The top row uses the rule based classifier. The bottom two rows use the neural network model trained on the original and stripped training sets respectively.

is a negative example for all other classes, and also that the quality of annotation is unsure, as in (Liu et al., 2003).

4.3 Neural Network Model

In addition to the two prior baselines, we model this problem using a neural network classifier.

Inspired by work in dataless classification (Chang et al., 2008), a key observation in this model is that each element in the output vector **y** represents a *document*, not just a label. Under this observation, we can create a meaningful representation for each label which gives an additional signal for classification. As such, we use the index i to retrieve c_i, and rewrite the decision function as $h_i(d, c_i) \rightarrow \{0, 1\}$. Ultimately, we define a single model for all $h_i(\cdot)$ as follows:

$$v_d = d2v(T(d)), \; v_d \in \mathbb{R}^{2k} \quad (1)$$
$$v_{c_i} = d2v(T(c_i)), \; v_{c_i} \in \mathbb{R}^{2k} \quad (2)$$
$$h_i(d, c_i) = f(v_d \odot v_{c_i}) \quad (3)$$

Where T is a token embedding function, $d2v$ is a document embedding function (with hidden states of size k), and f is a feed forward neural network layer that projects to two dimensions. Loosely speaking, the function h_i can be understood as measuring the similarity between the vector representations of d and c_i. We used allennlp to build our systems (Gardner et al., 2017). Our architecture is depicted in Figure 1.

For the token embedding layer T, we used the BERT base cased pretrained embeddings (Devlin et al., 2018), as provided by huggingface.[4] For the document embedding layer $d2v$, we used a bidirectional LSTM with hidden size 300, 2 layers,

and dropout 0.5. This embedder converts a sequence of embeddings into a fixed length by running the bidirectional LSTM over the sequence and concatenating the resulting context vectors from each direction. This document representation then has length equal to twice the hidden dimension of the LSTM, corresponding to the concatenation of the left and right context vectors.

We employed the same negative sampling and negative reweighting techniques for this model as described for the linear model.

4.4 Evaluation

During training, we tuned according to a split of the original train data. Since this data is automatically generated, it is not a good indicator of performance. Instead, we report all of our results on the manually annotated test set, described in Section 3.1. Since the decision from most of the classifiers will be 0, we evaluate the outputs of our model using F1 measure, calculated without regard to any individual class.

All of our code, data, and trained models are available online.[5]

5 Results and Analysis

Table 1 shows our main results. As expected, the rules-based approach gives high precision but low recall on the manually annotated set.

Interestingly, the linear and neural models trained on the original (unstripped) data achieve similar recall as the rule-based method, but suffer in precision. One explanation is that the imbalanced distribution of labels in the training set leads to overfitting of frequently-attested labels (hence the similar recall), and poor performance on all others (hence the drop in precision). The examples in Table 2 reinforce this idea.

Finally, the "stripped" results for each model show lower precision but higher recall relative to the original setting. We consider this an encouraging first step, which shows that the rule-stripping approach is important to prevent the model from simply re-learning deterministic training set rules. This pattern is particularly noticeable for the neural network model, which achieves the highest recall and highest overall performance of all approaches when trained on the "stripped" data.

In Table 2, we show some examples of pre-

Input sentence	Rule Pred.	NN Pred.
The defendant argued that their right to **free speech** had been chilled.	First Amendment	First Amendment
This was a **Second Amendment** case.	Second Amendment	Second Amendment
This was a **Ninth Amendment** case.	Ninth Amendment	Sixth Amendment, Eighth Amendment
The court argued that the punishment was not only cruel, but also unusual.	Unmatched	Eighth Amendment
The decision in Escobedo v. Illinois, 378 U.S. 478, stressed the need for protective devices to make the process of police interrogation conform to the dictates of the privilege.	Unmatched	Fifth Amendment

Table 2: A comparison of predictions from the rule-based system and the neural network model (stripped). The linear model is omitted to save space. **Bold text** represents text matching a rule. The three table sections correspond to examples on which 1) both models are correct 2) only rule-based is correct, and 3) only the neural network is correct. The last example is taken from the manually annotated test examples, with some formatting removed.

dictions from the rule-based system and the neural network model (the linear model is omitted to save space). The table has three sections, corresponding to examples on which 1) both models are correct, 2) only rule-based is correct, and 3) only the neural network is correct. The example from the second section ("Ninth Amendment case") is interesting in how it contrasts with the nearly identical sentence above it ("Second Amendment case"). Naturally, the rule-based system correctly tags both, but the neural network is only correct on the "Second Amendment" sentence. This is likely because of imbalances in the training data, such that sentences with the phrase "Second Amendment" are common, but sentences with the phrase "Ninth Amendment" are much less common. In fact, in the training split we used, the phrase "Ninth Amendment" appeared less than 10 times out of nearly 40K examples.

The bottom section shows the power of the neural network model. Words such as "cruel", "punishment", and "unusual" are distinctive of the Eighth Amendment, even though they are in a different order. Similarly, "the privilege" is a common shorthand for the Fifth Amendment's protections against self-incrimination ("No person [...] shall be compelled in any criminal case to be a witness against himself" → "the privilege against self-incrimination" → "the privilege"). Such examples are of particular interest to legal practitioners, but are difficult to capture in a rules-based framework.

6 Conclusions

We have introduced a new task for linking portions of text from Supreme Court cases to the US Constitution, some data supporting this task (although with incomplete annotations), and some baseline models, including a rule-based system, a linear model, and a neural network system. Although the neural network system outperforms both the rule-based and linear systems, there is still further exploration to be done both in the direction of automatic or distant labeling, and in problem modelling. We look forward to other researchers using this dataset for future work.

From a practical perspective, we anticipate that this dataset could be used to give valuable insights on research questions of interest to the world of political science. For example, these data could be used to study which amendments tend to see higher litigation rates according to the period in the Supreme Court, or rhetorical co-citation of Constitution sections.

Acknowledgments

This work was supported in part by a gift from Google and by contract HR0011-15-2-0025 with the US Defense Advanced Research Projects Agency (DARPA). The views expressed are those of the authors and do not reflect the official policy or position of the Department of Defense or the U.S. Government.

References

Matthew R Boutell, Jiebo Luo, Xipeng Shen, and Christopher M Brown. 2004. Learning multi-label scene classification. *Pattern recognition*, 37(9):1757–1771.

L Karl Branting. 2017. Data-centric and logic-based models for automated legal problem solving. *Artificial Intelligence and Law*, 25(1).5 27.

Pompeu Casanovas, Monica Palmirani, Silvio Peroni, Tom van Engers, and Fabio Vitali. 2016. Semantic web for the legal domain: the next step. *Semantic Web*, 7(3):213–227.

Ming-Wei Chang, Lev Ratinov, Dan Roth, and Vivek Srikumar. 2008. Importance of semantic representation: Dataless classification. In *AAAI*.

Jacob Devlin, Ming-Wei Chang, Kenton Lee, and Kristina Toutanova. 2018. Bert: Pre-training of deep bidirectional transformers for language understanding. *arXiv preprint arXiv:1810.04805*.

Daniel Duma and Ewan Klein. 2014. Citation resolution: A method for evaluating context-based citation recommendation systems. In *Proceedings of the 52nd Annual Meeting of the Association for Computational Linguistics (Volume 2: Short Papers)*, volume 2, pages 358–363.

Zachary Elkins, Tom Ginsburg, James Melton, Robert Shaffer, Juan F Sequeda, and Daniel P Miranker. 2014. Constitute: The worlds constitutions to read, search, and compare. *Journal of Web Semantics*, 27:10–18.

Matt Gardner, Joel Grus, Mark Neumann, Oyvind Tafjord, Pradeep Dasigi, Nelson F. Liu, Matthew Peters, Michael Schmitz, and Luke S. Zettlemoyer. 2017. Allennlp: A deep semantic natural language processing platform.

Bing Liu, Yang Dai, Xiaoli Li, Wee Sun Lee, and Philip S Yu. 2003. Building text classifiers using positive and unlabeled examples. In *Data Mining, 2003. ICDM 2003. Third IEEE International Conference on*, pages 179–186. IEEE.

Robert G McCloskey and Sanford Levinson. 2016. *The American supreme court*. University of Chicago Press.

Mike Mintz, Steven Bills, Rion Snow, and Dan Jurafsky. 2009. Distant supervision for relation extraction without labeled data. In *Proceedings of the Joint Conference of the 47th Annual Meeting of the ACL and the 4th International Joint Conference on Natural Language Processing of the AFNLP: Volume 2-Volume 2*, pages 1003–1011. Association for Computational Linguistics.

Jinseok Nam, Jungi Kim, Eneldo Loza Mencía, Iryna Gurevych, and Johannes Fürnkranz. 2014. Large-scale multi-label text classificationrevisiting neural networks. In *Joint european conference on machine learning and knowledge discovery in databases*, pages 437–452. Springer.

Tadashi Nomoto. 2018. Resolving citation links with neural networks. *Frontiers in Research Metrics and Analytics*, 3:31.

Lev Ratinov, Dan Roth, Doug Downey, and Mike Anderson. 2011. Local and global algorithms for disambiguation to wikipedia. In *Proceedings of the 49th Annual Meeting of the Association for Computational Linguistics: Human Language Technologies-Volume 1*, pages 1375–1384. Association for Computational Linguistics.

T Schwartz, M Berger, and J Hernandez. 2015. A legal citation recommendation engine using topic modeling and semantic similarity. In *Law and big data workshop, 15th international conference on artificial intelligence and law*.

Wei Shen, Jianyong Wang, and Jiawei Han. 2015. Entity linking with a knowledge base: Issues, techniques, and solutions. *IEEE Transactions on Knowledge and Data Engineering*, 27(2):443–460.

Litigation Analytics: Case outcomes extracted from US federal court dockets

Thomas Vacek[*], Ronald Teo[*], Dezhao Song[*], Conner Cowling[*] and Frank Schilder[*]
[*]Thomson Reuters R&D
610 Opperman Drive
Eagan, MN 55123, USA
`FName.LName@TR.com`

Timothy Nugent[†],
[†]Refinitiv
30 South Colonnade
Canary Wharf
London E145EP, UK
`FName.LName@Refinitiv.com`

Abstract

Dockets contain a wealth of information for planning a litigation strategy, but the information is locked up in semi-structured text. Manually deriving the outcomes for each party (e.g., settlement, verdict) would be very labor intensive. Having such information available for every past court case, however, would be very useful for developing a strategy because it potentially reveals tendencies and trends of judges and courts and the opposing counsel. We used Natural Language Processing (NLP) techniques and deep learning methods allowing us to scale the automatic analysis of millions of US federal court dockets. The automatically extracted information is fed into a Litigation Analytics tool that is used by lawyers to plan how they approach concrete litigations.

1 Introduction

This paper focuses on the creation of an index of *case outcomes* for a given docket, which we define as the legal procedure which resolves the case. By the nature of this definition, a case may have only one outcome. The case outcome is distinguishable from the outcomes for each party in the case, as some parties may be dismissed or receive judgment prior to the end of the case.

Dockets of US Federal Court cases contain the description of the various steps that lead to the overall outcome (e.g., settlement, verdict). The language describing these steps (i.e., filing a motion, an order by a judge, a dismissal) are not standardized among the various courts. In addition, the outcome is derived from a sequence of docket entries and requires global information.

The current work explores how various machine learning approaches can be used in order to solve the problem of assigning an outcome to a given docket. We start with an SVM approach inspired

#	Text
18	ORDER/NOTICE OF CHANGE IN COURT PROCEDURE. (Signed by Judge Marcia G. Cooke on 4/12/05) [EOD Date: 4/14/05] (lk) [Entry date 04/14/05]
19	AFFIDAVIT by Mohammed Vahid Re: [17-1] motion for summary judgment on the issue of liability (lk) [Entry date 06/20/05]
20	NOTICE of filing AFFIDAVIT by Mohammed Vahid Re: [17-1] motion for summary judgment on the issue of liability (lk) [Entry date 06/20/05]
21	MOTION with memorandum in support by Mohammed Vahid for summary judgment on the issue of liability (lk)
22	NOTICE of Unavailability by Maurice Gray Associa, Maurice Gray for dates of: 6/27/05 through 7/4/05 (lk) [Entry date 06/28/05]
23	NOTICE of acceptance of offer of judgment by Mohammed Vahid (lk) [Entry date 06/30/05]
24	VERIFIED MOTION by Mohammed Vahid for attorney fees, and to Tax Costs against the defendants pursuant to the provisions of the accepted offer of judgment and the fair labor standard act (lk) [Entry date 06/30/05]
25	NOTICE of filing Original Offer of Judgment and Plaintiff's notice of acceptance of offer of judgment by Mohammed Vahid (lk) [Entry date 06/30/05]
26	Certificate of Compliance pursuant to Local Rule 7.3 of the SDFL by Mohammed Vahid (lk) [Entry date 07/13/05]
27	EXPERT'S AFFIDAVIT by Maurice Gray Associa, Maurice Gray in support of [25-1] motion response (bb) [Entry date 07/28/05]
28	RESPONSE by Maurice Gray Associa, Maurice Gray to [23-1] motion for attorney fees, [23-2] motion to Tax Costs against the defendants pursuant to the provisions of the accepted offer of judgment and the fair labor standard act (bb) [Entry date 07/28/05]
29	REPLY by Mohammed Vahid to response to [23-1] motion for attorney fees, [23-2] motion to Tax Costs against the defendants pursuant to the provisions of the accepted offer of judgment and the fair labor standard act (lk) [Entry date 08/04/05]
30	NOTICE of Change of Address, telephone and Fax of attorney by Mohammed Vahid (lk) [Entry date 08/04/05]
31	CASE CLOSED. Case and Motions no longer referred to Magistrate. (lk) [Entry date 08/08/05]
32	ORDER denying as moot [17-1] motion for summary judgment on the issue of liability. (Signed by Judge Marcia G. Cooke on 8/5/05) [EOD Date: 8/8/05] (lk) [Entry date 08/08/05]

Figure 1: The final case outcome is *Settled*, as entry [23] indicates. Entries [19, 31, 32] are candidate entries for potential outcomes, but ultimately incorrect because of [23].

by (Nallapati and Manning, 2008), who developed an approach determining one specific procedure type (i.e., summary judgment). This approach does not take into account any sequence information, whereas the other two deep learning based approaches we utilized do. The first approach uses a CNN-GRU architecture based on the TF-IDF vectors created for each docket entry. The second approach is a simplified hierarchical RNN approach called Nested GRU modeling the words of each docket entry and using those for modeling the sequence of all docket entries in an RNN sequence model. Finally, an ensemble method via a GBM combines the outputs of all three classifiers

Proceedings of the Natural Legal Language Processing Workshop 2019, pages 45–54
Minneapolis, Minesotta, June 7, 2019. ©2019 Association for Computational Linguistics

in order to determine the final outcome.

Results show that the deep learning approaches outperform the SVM based approach, but there is no statistically significant difference between the two deep learning methods and the system that combines all three approaches. The combined system also provided the input for an actual system deployed to customers who utilize the analytics derived from the 8 million US Federal dockets for their litigation planning.

The US Federal Court system, including district trial courts, bankruptcy courts, and appellate courts, all use an electronic records system that provides public access via a government computer system called PACER (Public Access to Court Electronic Records). The system maintains databases giving metadata associations of parties to cases, attorneys to parties, filing and closing dates of the cases, related groups of filings, and a high-level outcome of each case. Pacer also holds the official record of the case, which is all the documents pertaining to the case filed by the parties, their counsel, and the court. In addition to the documents themselves, there is a concise summary of each document written by the filer (and in recent times, based on a generated suggested text created by template), as well as the record of events for which no record document exists such as minor hearings. We believe that the intricacy and nuance of court procedures, as well as attorneys' perception of how to use procedure to their clients' advantage, has and will continue to cause the court system to be resistant to the adoption of fully digital workflows. Thus, dockets will contain significant unstructured data for the foreseeable future, and the task of defining, extracting, and indexing important litigation events falls to third parties and requires NLP techniques.

The metadata outcome information from PACER and the case outcome that we seek to index are indeed similar. There are two reasons why the metadata element is not sufficient by itself: First, it is frequently inaccurate, apparently because of differences in interpretation among the clerks of different courts. Second, a more specific taxonomy can be defined and extracted.

Applying machine learning and NLP capabilities to all federal dockets allowed us to collect outcomes for almost 8 million past dockets and also enables us to keep up with all newly closed dockets. In addition to extracting the outcome, the system is able to accurately determine a small percentage of cases that are likely to have an inaccurate extracted outcome, which should be reviewed by a human.

The case outcome task is distinguishable from other classic problem formulations in the NLP space. Classical approaches to document classification fail for several reasons: First, distributional assumptions in document classification are not valid because parties can spend a great deal of effort on issues that ultimately have no bearing on the outcome of the case. For example, a docket may contain minutes of many days at trial, but the judgment was granted as a matter of law, indicated by a few terse words in the docket. Second, negation is frequently critical. For example, there are a significant number of docket entries which say something like, "Settlement conference held. Case not settled." Finally, the problem requires extraction of a large classes of related facts. For example, a great deal of time and effort may pass before a judge issues a ruling on a motion. In addition, even though the case outcome problem is inherently sequential, dockets don't satisfy the Markov assumption, as events can have skipping dependencies.

Figure 1,[1] for example, describes a case that ends with a settlement even though the last two entries simply state that the case was closed (i.e., dismissed) and all pending motions including a motion for summary judgment were dismissed. Based only on these entries, the case would be dismissed, but entry [23] contains language that points to a settlement without actually mentioning settlement, but the acceptance of an offer of judgment indicates this kind of outcome.

This paper describes in more detail how the problem of detecting the outcome for a case can be solved and provides an overview of how we utilized machine learning including deep learning capabilities in combination with manual review. First, we describe the background of the case outcome problem and previous work in this area in section 2. Then, we describe the overall solution architecture and the underlying machine learning approaches used in section 3. Section 4 provides more details on evaluating the different approaches. Section 5 outlines the content of a demo of the live system and section 6 concludes.

---

[1] Some entries are abbreviated for readability.

2 Background

2.1 Previous work

There have been only a few approaches that have dealt with information extraction and classification tasks of legal court proceedings. Nallapati and Manning (Nallapati and Manning, 2008) are one of the few researchers who investigated machine learning approaches applied to classifying summary judgment motions only. Their findings indicated that rule-based approaches showed better results than a machine learning approach such as using a Support Vector Machine (SVM) (Hearst, 1998). Their results indicated that a classification approach using an SVM with uni/bi-grams would achieve only an overall F1-value of about 0.8, while a specified rule-based approach is able to achieve almost 0.9 F1-value. In contrast to our approach they only used a docket entry classification for each docket entry. That is a component our system also has, but we complement the result from this component with two Deep Learning approaches. Their focus was also only on one motion type, whereas we determine the outcome of multiple outcomes including summary judgment. More generally, however, they sought to extract only granted summary judgment motions while our approach determines an outcome for all parties.

A more recent approach by (Vacek and Schilder, 2017) looks at a wider range of outcomes and uses a sequence tagging technique (i.e., CRF (Lafferty et al., 2001)) for determining the final outcome of a case for a party. The current work is an improvement over this approach in terms of performance and the set of outcome types is larger.

Related work has been presented by (Branting, 2017) addressing the issue of detecting errors in filing motions as well as the matching between motions and orders. He reports a mean rank of 0.5-0.6 on this task.

There has also been work on predicting the outcome of a court case based on the written decision (Aletras et al., 2016; Sulea et al., 2017). Those approaches take the opinion text into account and predict the ruling by the court (e.g. French Supreme Court). We focus on the information described in the dockets only. (Luo et al., 2017) propose an attention based neural network model for predicting charges based on the fact description alone. They also show that the neural network model outperforms an SVM based ap-

proach, but they do not rely on dockets descriptions. (Xiao et al., 2018) describe a large-scale challenge of predicting the charge, the relevant law article and the penalty for more than 5 million legal cases collected from the Supreme People's Court of China. Similar to one of our approaches, they use a CNN based approach to predict the outcome of a case. Although all of these recent outcome prediction approaches use similar neural network approaches, they do not base their prediction on dockets nor do they deal with the sequence information of different court actions as they are encoded in the court filings. Instead they base their predictions on the fact section of a written opinion. The problem definition differs from ours and we also cast a much wider net because many litigations are dismissed early and no court opinions are actually crafted for those cases.

Other work has focussed on the legal action for other courts such as the Delaware Court of Chancery (Badawi and Chen, 2017) or debt relief extracted from Bankruptcy court filings (Dobbie and Song, 2015).

3 Case outcomes

The system produces outcomes according to a hierarchical taxonomy. The top-level outcomes are dismissal by motion, dismissal without a motion (includes agreed dismissals), settlement, default judgment, summary judgment, verdict, and docketed elsewhere (a catch-all for transfer, consolidation, and remand.). For this paper, we evaluate only this top-level taxonomy; a finer taxonomy is desirable for most use cases, and our observation is that this can be accomplished by downstream steps that specialize each class. The population distribution of outcomes is highly imbalanced in favor of dismissals and settlements, with verdicts representing a very small percentage of outcomes. This is illustrated in Figure 2.

The overall architecture of the system should be understood in terms of two abstract steps, where each is implemented redundantly. The first step is the conditional analysis of a particular docket entry; the intent is to determine what outcomes the given entry would be consistent with, ie. $P(\text{entry}|\text{outcome})$. Note that estimating $P(\text{outcome}|\text{entry})$ is usually futile because outcomes have contextual dependencies on many entries. The second high-level step makes inferences based on the conditional evidence identified

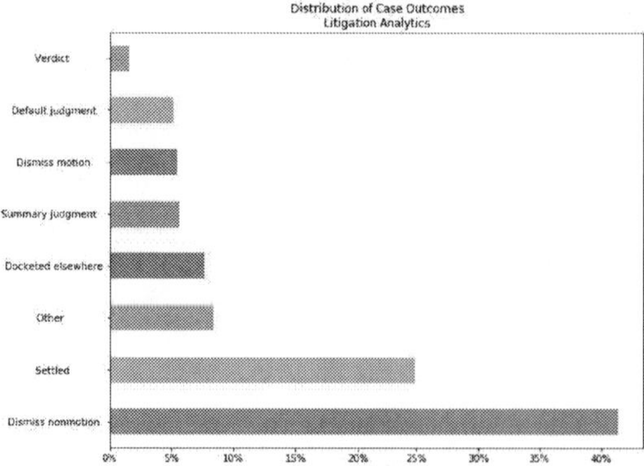

Figure 2: Federal cases are most likely settled or dismissed

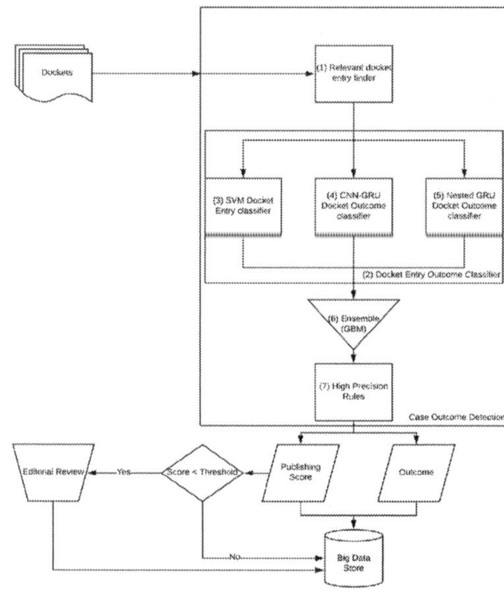

Figure 3: The overall architecture of the Case Outcome system

in the first step. This could be interpreted as using machine learning to determine the normalization and interactions in applying the Bayes rule to determine $P(\text{outcome}|\text{entry sequence})$. The interactions are important; some outcomes such as jury verdicts are expected to have a trail of consistent evidence such as trial records and post-trial motions, while others like settlement can come rather out of the blue. In the implemented system, some components (such as the SVM classifier) can be neatly categorized as one of these two steps. However, the deep learning methods implement both steps simultaneously. The system architecture is depicted in Figure 3.

There is one component of the system that we have omitted from discussion. The system makes use of a large number of business rules, which all can be neatly categorized into the first abstract step. The rules have the form of a terms-and-connectors search, requiring the conjunction of various conditions within a certain number of words. We omit discussion for two reasons: First, they require expert knowledge that cannot be imparted with any brevity. Second, they are less useful in the prediction task than one might suppose. The likely explanation is that for rare events, a small mis-estimation of $P(X|Y)$ (i.e. a rule that is too broad) would lead to a wildly incorrect estimate of $P(Y|X)$. These rules are useful, however, as a post-check of a predicted outcome; at least one entry can be expected to have a rule match implying high probability given the predicted outcome.

The high-level components are the following, as indicated in Figure 3:

1. A relevant docket entry finder. This module determines docket entries that are likely to have evidence as to the outcome of the docket. It is intended to have high recall, with little emphasis on precision.

2. A docket entry outcome classifier that predicts if a docket entry contains an outcome, and if so, which one. This classifier, similar to all the machine learning components, operates at the top level of the label taxonomy (see Figure 2). We developed three components to determine the final outcome of a docket.

3. An SVM was trained to provide an outcome per entry. Only the SVM approach uses the relevant docket entry.

4. A convolutional layer (CNN) followed by a Gated Recurrent Unit layer (GRU).

5. A nested recursive neural networks, one at the level of words in the docket entry and one at the level of docket entries.

6. A conventional gradient-boosted decision tree is used to predict the final outcome from features based on outcome SVM, CNN-GRU and Nested GRU classifier.

7. The next step applies human-written high-precision rules to sharpen the distinction be-

tween settlements and dismissals without a motion.

The final outcome is then localized (i.e., attached to a docket entry that gives evidence for it) using further rules that act on the docket closed date, the outcome entry classifier, and the outcome type classifier. Finally, the outcome is refined to add direction or open up the docketed elsewhere bucket using human-defined rules.

The output of the Docket Outcome component will provide the outcome as well as a confidence score. The confidence score is used for routing dockets either directly to the big data storage or to an editorial review system where cases and their outcomes are further reviewed by domain experts.

This paper will focus on the determination of a case outcome describing in more detail the components (3) SVM, (4) CNN-GRU, (5) Nested GRU, and (6) GBM.

3.1 Ensembling deep learning methods

In order to achieve high performance we ensembled various machine learning approaches including a SVM based approaches similar to (Nallapati and Manning, 2008). An SVM classifier focussing only on the outcome classification of the docket entry was trained in addition to two deep learning approaches.The first deep learning approach is a CNN-RNN combination that has a CNN (LeCun et al., 1998) layer followed by a GRU (Cho et al., 2014) layer before it is fed into a dense layer. The second deep learning approach is a nested RNN approach that first models each docket entry via an RNN (Schuster and Paliwal, 1997). Every docket entry is then the input for another RNN layer that models each docket entry as a step in the RNN model. The CNN-GRU and Nested-GRU model utilizes a custom trained word embeddings baed on Google's word2vec (Mikolov et al., 2013) to fine tune the embeddings to the docket corpus.

In the end, all scores retrieved from these models are used as features for a GBM (Friedman, 2000) model that combines the weights in order to determine the final outcome of the case.

SVM The purpose of this classifier is to predict the outcome associated with each entry of a docket. Note that this classifier does not take into account any interaction with previous outcomes or party information. The classifier used as input a feature vector for the top 3000 most frequent words/tokens, ordered by term frequency across the corpus words weighted by TF-IDF. A range of parameters were optimized including the maximum number of features (n=3000), the use of uni/bi-grams, lemmatization, removal of stop words, additive smoothing of IDF weights, sublinear term frequency scaling (i.e., $tf = 1 + log(tf)$), and regularizer choice. Some domain specific features were included such as binary encodings for the presence or absence of different party types, links etc, but these did not result in a significant performance improvement.

The classifier provides a robust prediction of whether an entry is consistent with one of the outcomes in scope. Often, however, the meaning of an entry can only be determined based on its context. A common example of this is when a lawsuit is dismissed because of technical but correctable deficiencies in the initial pleading. An explicit order dismissing the case may be followed shortly thereafter by a corrected complaint. Thus, the outcome of the case can only be determined by considering all of the entries in the docket, and more complex classifiers are required to determine the correct outcome of the docket as a whole. Hence, we incorporated two further deep learning models.

CNN-GRU In addition to predicting the associated outcome of each docket entry, we adopted a neural network based approach to predicting the outcome of one entire docket similar to (Wang et al., 2016). We first designed and experimented with a few Convolutional Neural Network (CNN) based approaches by adopting different architectures, e.g., single-input and multi-input (Yang and Ramanan, 2015) networks. In our single-input model, the input is vectorized features (e.g., word embeddings or TF-IDF scores) and we predict the outcome for each docket. When using word embeddings (our embedding has 300 dimensions), we concatenate all the docket entries and use the last 150 words (i.e., the input is a tensor with shape 150 * 300), since descriptions towards the end of a docket may be more indicative of the outcome. When using TF-IDF scores as the input, we first build a 322-word vocabulary by selecting words whose document frequency is above 20. Then, we use the last 150 docket entries and turn each docket entry into a 322-dimension vector (i.e., the input is a tensor with shape 150 * 322).

In our model, the input is first sent to a Convolutional layer and then a MaxPooling layer. Then, the intermediate results are sent to an GRU layer (a type of recurrent layers). At the bottom of our architecture, we use a Dense layer with softmax activation to obtain the final prediction. Differently, in our multi-input network, in addition to using the vectors (e.g., TF-IDF scores or word embeddings), we also utilize the output of the SVM classifier (i.e., the probabilities that a docket entry has certain outcomes) as additional input. By trying out different ways of combining these two inputs (e.g., combining them at the beginning of the network or running each input through a similar network and then combining them later), we found out that our multi-input model generally performs better than our single-input model.

Nested GRU The Nested GRU (cf. Figure 4) addressed the need to incorporate information from the entire sequence, as indicated by the docket excerpt in Figure 1. Compared to the SVM model, the Nested GRU is an end-to-end model that takes a matrix of shape (batch_size, MAX_ENTRIES, MAX_WORDS, EMBEDDING_SIZE) as input and produces a single outcome for the docket, which enables the network to learn directly from the docket outcome rather than the entry outcome that lacks all global information to determine the docket outcome. The Nested GRU utilizes the same idea of progressive encoding used by Hierarchical Attention Networks (HAN) as described by (Yang et al., 2016) but does not use an attention network to perform a "soft-search."

Using a hierarchical approach, we can preserve the natural structure of the docket (e.g., each entry consist of words and each docket consist of entries) for encoding. We summarize the "meaning" of each entry by encoding the sequence of words (e.g. "order granting motion," "consent order", "consent judgment") and propagate the encoding to the corresponding sequence to the next hierarchy consisting of GRU cells. This "docket entry level" hierarchy encodes the "meaning" of the entire docket and propagate the encoding to a fully-connected network with a softmax activation to obtain the classification of the entire docket.

GBM The system mediates the ensemble of predictors by means of a gradient boosted decision tree. The model takes an input of roughly 100 expert-designed features. For the ensemble predictors that solve the problem directly (deep learning models), obvious features arise, for instance, from the softmax probability estimate for each

outcome type. For ensemble predictors that have scope limited to a single docket entry (SVM and low-level patterns written for the manual-review flagging business rules discussed below), features are created from aggregations of the information extracted from each entry. The expert craft lies in how these aggregations are defined. Moreover, PACER provides limited metadata about the outcome of the case, so these factors can also be used to define various aggregations.

We treat the features generated by the SVM system (e.g., outcome probabilities) feeding into the GBM as the base system configuration. The experiments described in the next section will report on different combinations of the base system with the 2 deep learning approaches in order to keep the number of system combinations manageable.

3.2 Manual review

The output of party outcome detection may be flagged for manual review based on the prediction confidence scores output by the classifier and the numerous business rules mentioned previously. If an outcome is flagged, the docket is routed to an editorial tool that allows legal domain experts to review the extracted data. The automatically published and the reviewed dockets and their extracted motions/orders and outcomes are stored in a big data store.

4 Evaluation

4.1 Data

We sampled and acquired outcome annotations of 10,602 dockets. For each docket, one human annotator examined the entire docket and determined the outcome and associated docket entry for every party in the case. The case outcome, as defined for this task, is the last such outcome (for a party) in the case, assuming the case has been closed. A pre-study determined that overall inter-annotator agreement is relatively high with a kappa > 0.8. We used a fixed set of approximately 80% of the human annotated dockets for training and validation, and held out the remainder for testing.

The dataset used in this work is proprietary in accordance with the sponsor's requirements; however, an equivalent dataset could be acquired by any researcher inexpensively. Unannotated dockets can be obtained for free through the Free Law Project.[2] Moreover, courts can waive PACER fees

---

[2] http://free.law, also some of this collection has

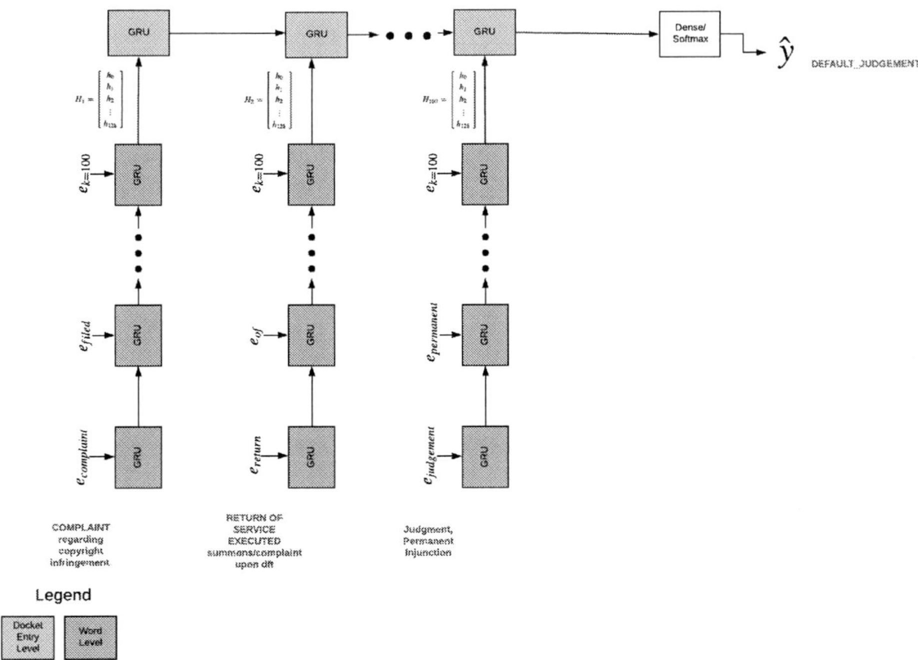

Figure 4: The sequence of words for each docket entries are nested into another layer of RNN modeling the sequence of entries

for research in the public interest.[3] Outcomes for these cases can be scraped from the Pacer Summary Report for $0.10 per case, or obtained for free with a fee waiver.

4.2 Experiments

We evaluated the overall system's performance by comparing how much the three different ML approaches contribute to the overall performance. Table 1 shows how the singular approaches behave. The nested GRU approach has the best overall performance and almost all individual outcomes are detected with higher F1-scores by this method (except for docketed elsewhere). The CNN-GRU methods shows better or equal results for each outcome compared to the results achieved by the SVM method we deployed.

We tested whether the performance of the respective system combinations are statistically different. We used the McNemar's test for identifying whether a machine learning classifier outperforms another one following the study by (Dietterich, 1998).

Table 3 indicates that the results created by the CNN-GRU and the Nested GRU approaches are significantly different from the baseline system that only uses SVM features for the GBM classification. The combined approach utilizing both CNN-GRU and Nested GRU features in addition to the SVM features outperforms the baseline system as well, but the performances of the CNN-GRU and Nested GRU looked at individually are not significantly different as indicated by the p-values obtained from the McNemar's test. There is also no statistically significant difference between the results of the combined approach and each of the results of the two deep learning approaches.

5 Demo

The outcome detection system described in this paper has been implemented in order to provide the case outcome information for all US federal judges and feeds into a Litigation Analytics program that allows lawyers to determine their litigation strategy. Lawyers can, for example, explore how often judges have ruled on a case resulting in a settlement, dismissal or trial. In addition, the

---

been uploaded to `http://archive.org`

[3]See Discretionary Fee Exemptions in the Pacer Fee Schedule at `https://www.pacer.gov/documents/` `epa_feesched.pdf`

	SVM			CNN-GRU			Nested GRU		
Outcome	Prec.	Recall	F1	Prec.	Recall	F1	Prec.	Recall	F1
DEFAULT JDG	0.79	0.85	0.81	0.85	0.85	0.85	0.92	0.92	0.92
DISMISS MOTION	0.90	0.81	0.85	0.94	0.83	0.88	0.90	0.89	0.90
DISMMISS	0.92	0.91	0.91	0.94	0.91	0.92	0.94	0.94	0.94
DOCKETED E.	0.88	0.85	0.86	0.88	0.85	0.86	0.90	0.79	0.84
OTHER	0.89	0.96	0.92	0.92	0.98	0.95	0.98	0.94	0.96
SETTLED	0.89	0.91	0.90	0.89	0.95	0.92	0.92	0.94	0.93
SUM JDG	0.87	0.82	0.84	0.89	0.89	0.89	0.89	0.89	0.89
VERDICT	0.69	0.71	0.70	0.79	0.65	0.71	0.72	0.76	0.74
Micro avg	0.88	0.88	0.88	0.90	0.90	0.90	0.91	0.91	0.91
Macro avg	0.85	0.85	0.85	0.88	0.86	0.87	0.90	0.88	0.89
Weighted avg	0.88	0.88	0.88	0.90	0.90	0.90	0.91	0.91	0.91

Table 1: Single approaches and respective performances

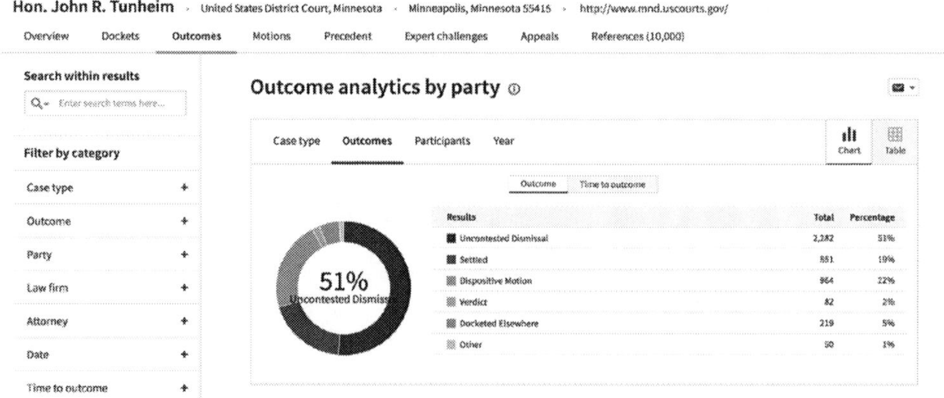

Figure 5: A screenshot of the Litigation Analytics system

Outcome	Prec.	Recall	F1
DEFAULT JDG	0.92	0.85	0.88
DISMISS MOTION	0.94	0.91	0.92
DISMMISS	0.93	0.93	0.93
DOCKETED E.	0.90	0.82	0.86
OTHER	0.96	0.96	0.96
SETTLED	0.92	0.94	0.93
SUM JDG	0.90	0.90	0.90
VERDICT	0.78	0.74	0.76
Micro avg	0.92	0.92	0.92
Macro avg	0.91	0.88	0.89
Weighted avg	0.92	0.92	0.92

Table 2: Results of all approaches combined

	CNN-GRU	Nested	All
SVM	**0.013**	**0.002**	**0.000**
CNN-GRU		0.256	0.071
Nested			0.549

Table 3: P-values for the McNemar's test for system combinations

user can determine how long it takes for a particular judge to reach a settlement etc.

Figure 5 indicates what the distribution of different high level outcomes is for the federal Judge John Tunheim. The user can then further explore the outcomes and identify more fine-grained outcomes. Furthermore, they can select further categories such as law firms, parties, attorneys or simple date restrictions in order to research similar cases that would inform them regarding their best strategy for their clients.

6   Conclusion

We have described how to extract the case outcome from the docket entry summaries, and provided justification for why this task is important. While the system is very accurate for the scope of the defined task, the future challenges almost all revolve around making sure that the metadata events in this large-scale case catalog are relevant, accurate, unbiased, and useful. For example, it is critical to ensure that the mistakes of the system are unbiased as to the selection criteria that a user might wish to study. We use audits, user feedback, and specific queries to investigate the accuracy of outcomes.

More generally, determining what legal events in a case should be detected and indexed requires considerable collaboration between legal experts and NLP experts. The definition of "case outcome" as we have used it here was the result of a great deal of investigation and consultation. There are many additional events that could be extracted.

Finally, the system described here relies entirely on the concise summaries of the events of the case described in the docket entries, while ignoring the official record documents themselves. This is due, in part, to the difficulty in large-scale access to those documents. Access to the records of the case would open the possibility to track *issue outcomes*, or the success of failure of each claim in a case instead of the case as a whole.

References

Nikolaos Aletras, Dimitrios Tsarapatsanis, Daniel Preotiuc-Pietro, and Vasileios Lampos. 2016. Predicting judicial decisions of the European Court of Human Rights: a Natural Language Processing perspective. *PeerJ Computer Science*, 2:e93.

Adam B Badawi and Daniel L Chen. 2017. The Shareholder Wealth Effects of Delaware Litigation. *American Law and Economics Review*, 19(2):287–326.

Luther Karl Branting. 2017. Automating judicial document analysis. In *Proceedings of the Second Workshop on Automated Semantic Analysis of Information in Legal Texts co-located with the 16th International Conference on Artificial Intelligence and Law (ICAIL 2017), London, UK, June 16, 2017.*

Kyunghyun Cho, Bart van Merrienboer, Dzmitry Bahdanau, and Yoshua Bengio. 2014. On the properties of neural machine translation: Encoder-decoder approaches. In *Proceedings of SSST@EMNLP 2014, Eighth Workshop on Syntax, Semantics and Structure in Statistical Translation, Doha, Qatar, 25 October 2014*, pages 103–111.

Thomas G. Dietterich. 1998. Approximate statistical tests for comparing supervised classification learning algorithms. *Neural Computation*, 10(7):1895–1923.

Will Dobbie and Jae Song. 2015. Debt relief and debtor outcomes: Measuring the effects of consumer bankruptcy protection. *American Economic Review*, 105(3):1272–1311.

Jerome H. Friedman. 2000. Greedy function approximation: A gradient boosting machine. *Annals of Statistics*, 29:1189–1232.

Marti A. Hearst. 1998. Trends & controversies: Support vector machines. *IEEE Intelligent Systems*, 13(4):18–28.

John D. Lafferty, Andrew McCallum, and Fernando C. N. Pereira. 2001. Conditional random fields: Probabilistic models for segmenting and labeling sequence data. In *Proceedings of the Eighteenth International Conference on Machine Learning (ICML 2001), Williams College, Williamstown, MA, USA, June 28 - July 1, 2001*, pages 282–289.

Yann LeCun, Léon Bottou, Yoshua Bengio, and Patrick Haffner. 1998. Gradient-based learning applied to document recognition. *Proceedings of the IEEE*, 86(11):2278–2324.

Bingfeng Luo, Yansong Feng, Jianbo Xu, Xiang Zhang, and Dongyan Zhao. 2017. Learning to predict charges for criminal cases with legal basis. *CoRR*.

Tomas Mikolov, Ilya Sutskever, Kai Chen, Gregory S. Corrado, and Jeffrey Dean. 2013. Distributed representations of words and phrases and their compositionality. In *Advances in Neural Information Processing Systems 26: 27th Annual Conference on Neural Information Processing Systems 2013. Proceedings of a meeting held December 5-8, 2013, Lake Tahoe, Nevada, United States.*, pages 3111–3119.

Ramesh Nallapati and Christopher D Manning. 2008. Legal docket-entry classification: Where machine learning stumbles. In *Proceedings of the Conference on Empirical Methods in Natural Language Processing*, pages 438–446, Honolulu, Hawaii. Association for Computational Linguistics, Association for Computational Linguistics.

Mike Schuster and Kuldip K. Paliwal. 1997. Bidirectional recurrent neural networks. *IEEE Trans. Signal Processing*, 45(11):2673–2681.

Octavia-Maria Sulea, Marcos Zampieri, Shervin Malmasi, Mihaela Vela, Liviu P. Dinu, and Josef van Genabith. 2017. Exploring the use of text classification in the legal domain. *CoRR*, abs/1710.09306.

Tom Vacek and Frank Schilder. 2017. A sequence approach to case outcome detection. In *Proceedings of the 16th edition of the International Conference on Articial Intelligence and Law*, pages 209–215. ACM.

Xingyou Wang, Weijie Jiang, and Zhiyong Luo. 2016. Combination of convolutional and recurrent neural network for sentiment analysis of short texts. In *Proceedings of COLING 2016, the 26th International Conference on Computational Linguistics: Technical Papers*, pages 2428–2437, Osaka, Japan. The COLING 2016 Organizing Committee.

Chaojun Xiao, Haoxi Zhong, Zhipeng Guo, Cunchao Tu, Zhiyuan Liu, Maosong Sun, Yansong Feng, Xianpei Han, Zhen Hu, Heng Wang, and Jianfeng Xu. 2018. CAIL2018: A large-scale legal dataset for judgment prediction. *CoRR*, abs/1807.02478.

Songfan Yang and Deva Ramanan. 2015. Multi-scale recognition with dag-cnns. In *2015 IEEE International Conference on Computer Vision, ICCV 2015, Santiago, Chile, December 7-13, 2015*, pages 1215–1223.

Zichao Yang, Diyi Yang, Chris Dyer, Alex Smola, and Eduard Hovy. 2016. Hierarchical attention networks for document classification. In *Proceedings of NAACL 2016*, pages 1480–1489.

Developing and Orchestrating a Portfolio of Natural Legal Language Processing and Document Curation Services

Georg Rehm[1], Julián Moreno-Schneider[1], Jorge Gracia[2], Artem Revenko[3], Victor Mireles[3], Maria Khvalchik[3], Ilan Kernerman[4], Andis Lagzdins[5], Marcis Pinnis[5], Arturs Vasilevskis[5], Elena Leitner[1], Jan Milde[1], Pia Weißenhorn[1]

[1]DFKI GmbH, Germany; [2]University of Zaragoza, Spain;
[3]Semantic Web Company, Austria; [4]K Dictionaries, Israel; [5]Tilde, Latvia

Corresponding author: `georg.rehm@dfki.de`

Abstract

We present a portfolio of natural legal language processing and document curation services currently under development in a collaborative European project. First, we give an overview of the project and the different use cases, while, in the main part of the article, we focus upon the 13 different processing services that are being deployed in different prototype applications using a flexible and scalable microservices architecture. Their orchestration is operationalised using a content and document curation workflow manager.

1 Introduction

We present a portfolio of various Natural Legal Language Processing and Document Curation services currently under development in the collaborative EU project LYNX, in which a consortium of partners from academia and industry develops a platform for the easier and more efficient processing of documents from the legal domain. First, our platform is acquiring data and documents related to compliance from multiple jurisdictions in different languages with a focus on Spanish, German, Dutch, Italian and English, along with terminologies, dictionaries and other language resources. Based on this collection of structured data and unstructured documents we create the multilingual Legal Knowledge Graph (LKG). Second, a set of flexible language processing services is developed to analyse and process the data and documents to integrate them into the LKG. Semantic processing components annotate, structure, and interlink the LKG contents. The LKG is incrementally augmented by linking to external data sets, by discovering topics and entities linked implicitly, as well

as by using machine translation services to provide access to documents, previously unavailable, in certain languages. Finally, three pilots are developed that exploit the LKG in industry use cases.

The remainder of this article is structured as follows. Section 2 describes the different use cases, while, in the main part of the article (Section 3), we focus upon the 13 different processing services used in the prototype applications . The orchestration of the services is operationalised using a content and document curation workflow manager (Section 4). After a brief review of related work (Section 5) we summarise the article and take a look at future work (Section 6).

2 Use Cases

Within LYNX we work with three different use cases embedded in use case scenarios. In the following, we briefly sketch the three use cases.

The objective of the *contract analysis* use case is to enhance compliance with data protection obligations through automation, reducing costs, corporate risks and personal risks. The prototype analyses data protection legislation and case law from the EU and Member States and contracts between controllers, data subjects, processors, data processing policies and general contracts.

The *labour law* use case provides access to aggregated and interlinked legal information regarding labour law across multiple legal orders, jurisdictions, and languages. The prototype analyses labour legislation from the EU and Member States, and jurisprudence related to labour law issues.

The *oil and gas* use case is focused on compliance management support for geothermal energy projects and aims to obtain standards and regulations associated with certain terms in the field of

55

Proceedings of the Natural Legal Language Processing Workshop 2019, pages 55–66
Minneapolis, Minesotta, June 7, 2019. ©2019 Association for Computational Linguistics

geothermal energy. A user can submit a RFP or feasibility study to the system and is then informed which standards or regulations must be taken into consideration to carry out the considered project in a compliant manner. This scenario will innovate and speed up existing compliance related services.

3 NLLP Services

In the following main part of this article we describe many of the Natural Legal Language Processing services currently under development in our project: Term Extraction (Section 3.1), Lexical Resources (Section 3.2), Named Entity Recognition (Section 3.3), Concept Extraction (Section 3.4), Word Sense Disambiguation (Section 3.5), Temporal Expression Analysis (Section 3.6), Legal Reference Resolution (Section 3.7), Text Structure Recognition (Section 3.8), Text Summarisation (Section 3.9), Machine Translation (Section 3.10), Legal Knowledge Graph Population (Section 3.11), Semantic Similarity (Section 3.12) and Question Answering (Section 3.13). This set of services is heterogeneous: some of the services make use of other services, some services extract or annotate information (e. g., NER or Temporal Expression Analysis), while others operate on full documents (e. g., summarisation or machine translation), yet others provide a user interface (e. g., QA).

3.1 Term Extraction

To enable the creation of a taxonomy for a certain use case, domain or company, we use the cloud-based Tilde Terminology term extraction service[1]. It extracts terms from different corpora following the methodology by Pinnis et al. (2012). As a result, the platform creates a SKOS vocabulary containing terms, contexts and references to their source documents. Each term comes with a ranking score to describe the terms specificity in the source corpora compared to a general language corpus. The score is calculated based on TF-IDF (Spärck Jones, 1972) and co-occurrence statistics for multi-word terms (Pinnis et al., 2012). Once the term extraction workflow has been triggered, a corresponding online platform takes over. The workflow starts with plain text extraction from different file formats, then all plain-text documents are annotated, and a single collection of terms is created. As multiple surface forms of the same term may appear in the text, term normalisation is performed. This term collection is the first step towards, initially, creating or, later on, enriching the Legal Knowledge Graph. The collection can be used for creating hierarchical taxonomies augmented with multilingual information and linked to other knowledge bases.

3.2 Lexical Resources for the Legal Domain

An essential aspect of the LKG is its capability to be easily adaptable across domains and sectors. It is based on both domain-dependent and domain-independent vocabularies, which will be accessible through a common RDF graph. The domain-dependent vocabularies account for particular terminologies coming from the legal sector and our use case domains (e. g., EuroTermBank[2]). The domain-independent vocabularies are taken from families of monolingual, bilingual and multilingual dictionaries published by one of our project partners, such as Global, Password, and Random House.[3] They contain various cross-lingual links for the five languages served by our platform (Dutch, English, German, Italian, Spanish). Besides their overall coverage of solely domain-independent vocabularies, they contain information on words and phrases that include also or only domain-dependent meanings (e. g., court for the former, lawyer for the latter). The motivation of relying on domain-independent dictionary data for the LKG is thus twofold: first, they provide a common substrate across domains that facilitates traversing semantically annotated documents coming from different specialised domains (e. g., Legal or Oil & Gas); second, they support certain NLP functionalities such as Word Sense Disambiguation and Word Sense Induction by providing a common catalogue of word senses. The data is being remodeled in RDF according to the Ontolex Lemon Lexicography Module Specification[4] and is accessed by the platform via a RESTful API. The LKG has a common core part (terminologies, sets of annotated legal corpora), but can be expanded to accommodate the necessities of particular use cases (e. g., to store private contracts).

---

[1] https://term.tilde.com

[2] http://www.eurotermbank.com

[3] https://www.lexicala.com

[4] https://jogracia.github.io/ontolex-lexicog/

3.3 Named Entity Recognition

The service for named entity recognition (NER) includes the elaboration of corresponding semantic classes and the preparation of a German language data set. Several state of the art models were trained, i. e., Conditional Random Fields (CRFs) and bidirectional Long-Short Term Memory Networks (BiLSTMs), and evaluated (Finkel et al., 2005; Faruqui and Padó, 2010; Benikova et al., 2014, 2015; Huang et al., 2015; Lample et al., 2016; Riedl and Padó, 2018, etc.). For training and evaluating the system we used a data set of German court decisions that was manually annotated with seven coarse-grained and 19 fine-grained classes: names and citations of people (person, judge, lawyer), location (country, city, street, area), organisation (organisation, company, institution, court, brand), legal norm (law, legal regulation, European legal norm), case-by-case regulation (regulation, contract), case law, and legal literature. The data set consists of approximately 67,000 sentences and around 54,000 annotated entities. For the experiment, two tools for sequence labeling were chosen. These are sklearn-crfsuite (CRFs)[5] and UKPLab-BiLSTM (BiLSTMs)[6] (Reimers and Gurevych, 2017). Three different models and two classifications each are developed for each of these model families (19 and seven classes, respectively). For CRFs these are (1) CRF-F with features, (2) CRF-FG with features and gazetteers, (3) CRF-FGL with features, gazetteers, and the lookup table. For BiLSTMs we used (1) BiLSTM-CRF without character embeddings, (2) BiLSTM-CRF+, and (3) BiLSTM-CNN-CRF with character embeddings generated by BiLSTM and by a CNN. In order to reliably estimate the performance of the models, we use stratified 10-fold cross-validation, which prevents overfitting during training. The stratification guarantees that the semantic classes are equally frequent in the test set relative to the size of the training set, which avoids measurement errors in the case of unbalanced data. The results were measured with precision, recall, and F_1-measure. The BiLSTM models performed better compared to CRF (see Table 1), the F_1 values were between 93.75–95.46 % for the fine-grained classes and

between 94.68–95.95 % for the coarse-grained classes. By contrast, the CRF models reached 93.05–93.23 % and 93.11–93.22 %. Overall, the CRF models achieved about 1–10 % lower scores per class than the BiLSTMs. The models provide the best results in the fine-grained classes of judges, courts and laws; their F_1 values were 95 %. Performance was an F_1 value over 90 % in the classes countries, institutions, case laws and legal literature. The recognition of the classes persons, lawyers, cities, companies, legal regulations, European legal norms and contracts varied from 84 % to 93 %. In contrast, the values in the classes streets, landscapes, organisations and regulations were the lowest and amounted to 69–80 % with the CRF models and to 72–83 % with BiLSTM. The worst result was observed in the class brands. With CRF, a maximum F_1 value of 69.61 % was reached and with BiLSTM a maximum F_1 value of 79.17 %. The current NER tool is a working prototype. It already provides named entities locally, but is still being evaluated further. As of now, the service is available for German texts, but it can be easily adapted to other languages.

3.4 Concept Extraction

The LKG contains among its nodes entities from controlled vocabularies. These are typically expressed as SKOS concepts, which permits assigning to them multiple labels, i. e., various surface forms, in multiple languages. Furthermore, one can define relations between instances of concepts, such as hypernymy, to create a taxonomy. Taxonomies become useful when their concepts can be identified in documents, a process called Concept Extraction. A simple example would be taking the sentence "The tenants must pay the heating costs by themselves", and identifying the presence of the concepts "tenant" and "heating costs". If these are known to be instances of *Contractual parties* and *Energy costs*, respectively, a search for "energy costs" would point the user to this sentence. Thus, once concept extraction is performed, links between documents and elements of controlled vocabularies in the LKG can be established. While these relations are rather simple, they are the first step for enriching text fragments with knowledge from the LKG, as well as to enable further algorithms for the (semi-)automatic extension of the LKG. Importantly, the inclusion of labels in many languages allows linking of

---

[5] https://sklearn-crfsuite.readthedocs.io/en/latest/

[6] https://github.com/UKPLab/emnlp2017-bilstm-cnn-crf

Table 1: F_1 values of the CRF and BiLSTM models for the coarse-grained classes.

Class	CRFs			BiLSTMs		
	F	FG	FGL	CRF	CRF+	CNN-CRF
Person	91.74	**92.20**	92.16	94.74	**95.41**	95.12
Location	89.26	89.45	**90.18**	91.68	**93.31**	92.57
Organisation	90.87	90.99	**91.11**	91.37	92.87	**93.21**
Legal norm	95.67	95.77	**95.86**	96.77	**97.98**	97.79
Case-by-case regulation	86.94	**86.96**	86.39	85.43	**90.61**	90.43
Case law	93.23	**93.25**	93.08	96.56	**96.99**	96.78
Legal literature	91.92	92.06	**92.11**	93.84	**94.42**	94.02
Total	93.11	**93.22**	93.22	94.68	**95.95**	95.79

documents in different languages, combining the knowledge derived from them, as well as multilingual search and recommendation. The Concept Extraction service works in as many languages as the taxonomies have labels in, and thus we can leverage multinational efforts for creating multilingual taxonomies such as EUROVOC[7] or UNBIS[8]. Furthermore, in the case where documents are in English, Spanish, Dutch, German, French, Italian, Czech or Slovak languages, additional linguistic processing increases the recall. The service can be used for production. It is available in most European languages.

3.5 Word Sense Disambiguation

To enable the use of incomplete KGs for automatic text annotations, we introduce a robust method for discriminating word senses using thesaurus information like hypernyms, synonyms, types/classes, which is contained in the KG. The method uses collocations to induce word senses and to discriminate the thesaurus sense from others. Its main novelty is using thesaurus information already at the stage of sense induction. The given KG enables us to cast the task to a binary scenario, namely telling apart the KG sense from all the others. This method does not require all possible senses of a word to be contained in the KG, which makes it especially useful in a production environment, where usually only incomplete KGs are available. We take as input a corpus, thesaurus information, and a concept from the KG, one of whose labels is found throughout the corpus (the target label). We want to distinguish, for each document in the data set, whether the target label is used in the thesaurus sense or not.[9] Thus, the

Table 2: Cocktails WSID accuracy scores

	Macro average	Micro average
Our Method	0.841	0.896
Baseline	0.725	0.737

Table 3: MeSH WSID accuracy scores

	Macro average	Micro average
Our Method	0.723	0.739
Baseline	0.680	0.735

end result is a partition of the corpus into two disjoint collections: "this" and "other". The collection "this" contains the documents that feature the target label in the thesaurus sense, the collection "other" contains any other sense which does not match the domain captured in the thesaurus, which can be more than one. The experiments were conducted on two data sets[10] created specifically for this task: Cocktails and MeSH (Revenko and Mireles, 2017) (Table 3). This service is used for any kind of entity linking, especially after NER. This is done to correctly identify which named entities are indeed within the vocabulary scope of the LKG. The service is a working prototype. It is language agnostic, i.e., works for any language as long as the text can be tokenised correctly.

3.6 Temporal Expression Analysis

Documents from the legal domain contain a multitude of temporal expressions that can be analysed, normalised (i.e., semantically interpreted) and further exploited for document and information mining purposes. We implemented a prototype for the analysis of time expressions in German-language legal documents, especially court decisions and legislative texts. Temporal expressions

---

[7] https://publications.europa.eu/en/web/eu-vocabularies/

[8] http://metadata.un.org/?lang=en

[9] Without loss of completeness we consider only the case when the target label is used in the same sense in all occurrences in a document. One can, of course, consider the context of every occurrence of the target label as a separate document, therefore extending the method to disambiguate every single occurrence of the target label.

[10] https://github.com/artreven/thesaural_wsi

Table 4: Comparison of the results of the original version of HeidelTime (HT) with the modified (HT nV) on the evaluation corpus. The last line indicates the improvement.

	strict			partial			strict+value				partial+value			
	P	R	F1	P	R	F1	P	R	F1	Acc	P	R	F1	Acc
HT	86.8	86.0	86.4	89.5	88.1	88.8	86.1	85.3	85.7	99.2	88.4	87.1	87.8	98.9
HTnV	94.9	92.0	93.5	96.6	93.5	95.0	94.0	91.1	92.5	99.0	95.3	92.3	93.8	98.7
+	8.2	6.1	7.1	7.1	5.4	6.2	7.9	5.8	6.9	0.2	6.9	5.1	6.0	0.2

include dates, e. g., "1. Januar 2000" (1st January 2000), durations, e. g., "fünf Kalenderjahre" (five calendar years) and repeating time intervals, e. g., "jeden Monat" (every month). Such expressions should not only be identified, but also normalised by translating them into a standardised ISO format. Since no suitable data set existed, a text collection was prepared and annotated with temporal expressions using the TimeML standard. Previously, the automatic identification of temporal expressions (temporal tagging) has been mainly focused on English and domains such as news and narrative texts. Research showed that this task is domain- and language-sensitive, i. e., systems have to be adapted to the specific domain or language to ensure consistent performance. We can confirm this observation: during the annotation of the corpus deficits had become apparent, which concerned not only the annotation guidelines, but also the performance of the rule-based temporal tagger HeidelTime (Strötgen and Gertz, 2010), which was subsequently extended. One of the specifics of the domain are references to other legal texts which contain (alleged) dates ("Richtlinie 2008 / 96 /EG", "Directive 2008 / 96 /EG"). Other peculiarities of the domain and/or language are the frequent use of compounds such as "Kalenderjahr" (calendar year), "Fälligkeitsmonat" (due month) or "Bankarbeitstag" (banking day), generic use of temporal expressions such as "jeweils zum 1. Januar" (1st January of each year) and event-anchored temporal expressions "Tag der Verkündigung" (proclamation day). Based on our new annotated corpus, HeidelTime was adapted to the domain. The evaluation showed that the adjustments made to HeidelTime significantly improved its performance (Table 4. Particularly noteworthy is the recall with an increase of approx. 10 percentage points. Normalisation remains problematic, which is also due to generic or event-based uses of temporal expressions as well as legal references.

3.7 Legal Reference Resolution

References to other documents are another class of expressions used in abundance in documents from the legal domain. The considered problem consists in recognizing and, ideally resolving, such references. Usually, editors attempt to be consistent and follow patterns to reference other documents. The developed methodology, currently implemented as a language-agnostic prototype, follows this assumption and attempts to discover patterns used in a semi-automatic manner. The discovered patterns are constructed from features that are either individual tokens (e. g., "Decision", "EU", etc.) or processed features (e. g., "DIGITS" as a placeholder for numbers). We use a seed collection of documents, where references have been manually annotated and resolved. For each reference we collect the tokens preceding the reference and analyse the features present in these tokens. Next we aggregate the most common combinations of features – these form "patterns". Example of a pattern could be {"EU", "Decision", "DIGITS/DIGITS"} or {"the", "data", "subject"}. The second pattern is an example of a common combinations of tokens in text and does not necessarily indicate a reference. To filter out such irrelevant patterns from the seed documents we extract the strings containing the candidate pattern, but not containing a reference. If several such strings are found the pattern is discarded. In the next step the most common undiscarded patterns are presented to the user who can accept several patterns that are later used to discover new references, enabling the recursive improvement of patterns.

3.8 Text Structure Recognition

Knowing the structure of a document can drastically improve the performance of the analysis services applied to the text, as specialised fine-grained models and focused approaches can be integrated. In the legal domain, it is important to determine the structure of a document to identify sections, subsections, paragraphs, etc. correctly because many legal references also contain this type of information, ideally enabling automatically linking to the correct part of the text, instead of the whole document. Robust text structure recognition is still an open research question. Many approaches have been suggested in different fields, such as Optical Layout Recognition (OLR) for unstructured documents or markup-based approaches for structured documents. We try to cover both in our prototype.

Unstructured documents do not contain any structure information whatsoever, they are often provided in plain text. To process (plain) text, we start by applying a pattern based approach (regular expressions) that allows the identification of the title, headings and running text or paragraphs. After that, we apply topic detection to all those parts (both titles and running texts) in order to cluster sections with related topics.

Structured documents include structural information (e. g., markup). We consider two ways of analysing them: (1) defining a mapping between the elements important and relevant for the use cases addressed by our platform and the structural elements of the documents; and (2) extracting the plain text from the document and then applying the techniques for unstructured documents.

3.9 Text Summarisation

To enable our users to work with legal documents more efficiently, we experiment with summarisation services (Allahyari et al., 2017). While extractive summarisation has been popular in the past, the progress in neural technologies has renewed the interest in abstractive summarisation, i. e., generating new sentences that capture a document's meaning. This approach requires highly complex models and a lot of training data. In the absence of labeled training data, extractive methods are often used as the basis for abstractive methods, by assigning relevance scores to sentences in an unsupervised way. Abstractive summarisation is often augmented using word embeddings (Mikolov et al., 2013; Pennington et al., 2014) that provide a shared semantic space for those strongly related sentences that do no share the same but similar or related words. We develop two methods. The first tool is based on TF-IDF (Neto et al., 2000). This is a popular baseline as it is easy to implement, unsupervised, and language independent. Instead of using bag-

of-words sentence representations, our approach tries to improve on this, by analysing the texts first. Searching the embedding space of all words used in the text, we cluster similar words so that morphological variants of a word like "tree" and "trees" or "eat" and "eating", but also synonyms like "fast" and "rapid" are considered as belonging to the same cluster. Based on these groupings we encode all documents and then calculate the weights for the sentences using TF-IDF. The second tool is based on the concept of centroids (Rossiello et al., 2017; Ghalandari, 2017) and benefits from the composability of word embeddings. Initially, keywords and concepts are extracted from the document. By composing their embeddings, the centroid is created, which represents the document's condensed meaningful information. It is then projected into the embedding space together with all sentence embeddings. Sentences receive relevance scores depending on their distance to the centroid in the embedding space. To avoid redundancy in the summary, sentences that are too similar to the ones already added to the summary are not used. Both tools can be used for multiple languages, single and multi-document summarisation. The current version of the centroid text summarisation is a working prototype. It already provides extractive summaries for single and multiple documents, but is still being tested and optimised. The service is only available for English but can be adapted to other languages by training new embeddings.

3.10 Machine Translation

To enable multilingualism and cross-lingual extraction, linking and search, we use the Machine Translation (MT) service Tilde MT[11]. In order to populate and process the Legal Knowledge Graph in a multilingual way, custom Neural Machine Translation (NMT) systems were trained for selected language pairs – English ↔ Spanish, English ↔ German, and English ↔ Dutch. In-domain business case specific legal data was gathered and processed prior to training the NMT systems on a mix of broad-domain and in-domain data to be able to translate both in-domain and out-of-domain texts. Marian was used for training (Junczys-Dowmunt et al., 2018). The translation service provides support for a runtime scenario as well as for asynchronous processes, i. e., support-

---

[11]`https://tilde.com/mt`

Table 5: Evaluation results of NMT systems

Language pair	Sentence pairs	BLEU	
		to EN	from EN
English ↔ Dutch	41,639,299	43.54	34.12
English ↔ Spanish	81,176,632	32.52	38.36
English ↔ German	24,768,821	38.73	44.73

ing background data curation processes. The synchronous translation service endpoint serves translation functionality for texts and documents annotated with the Natural Language Processing Interchange Format ontology (NIF) (Hellmann et al., 2013). The systems were automatically evaluated using BLEU (Papineni et al., 2002) on held-out evaluation sets. The sets were created from the in-domain parts of the parallel corpora used for training of the NMT systems. Table 5 contains statistics of the training data and the automatic evaluation results of the NMT systems.

3.11 Legal Knowledge Graph Population

For the definition of our Knowledge Graph, we benefit from predefined vocabularies such as EUROVOC. However, their knowledge is limited to that intended by their creators, and their level of specificity and focus will, in general, not match the ones required for an application. One possible option of extending existing knowledge resources is the large-scale analysis of documents in which entities contained in the knowledge resources have been identified, and to identify as well as to extract new relations, claims, or facts, explicitly mentioned in the documents. This approach mimics the process in which a human reads and understands documents. In our project we follow distant supervision (Ren et al., 2017). It takes a text corpus as input and 1) identifies sentences containing entity pairs for which relations are known, 2) uses machine learning to derive a statistical classifier to recognize these examples, and 3) applies this classifier to sentences that, by virtue of the classes of entities they contain, could also include an instance of a relation. The result is a list of sentences which have been annotated as containing a given relation. The relations included so far in this first experimental deployment, are of the type *person is located in location* and *location is contained in location*. They will be expanded with domain specific relations such as *activity requires permit* or *permit was issued on date*. So far, such relations can be recognized in English language texts, but training for German, Spanish and Dutch, using the

same distant supervision approach is possible due to the multilingual nature of general purpose corpora and knowledge graphs (e. g., DBPedia).

3.12 Semantic Similarity

Using the services mentioned above, documents in the LKG are annotated to semantically describe their content and provenance. This added extra knowledge is useful for several applications, such as search, question answering, classification and recommendations, all of which rely on a notion of document similarity. Many such notions exist, and they are usually encoded in a function s that assigns, to every pair of documents, a number between 0 and 1, with 1 denoting the documents being identical (Gomaa and Fahmy, 2013). We use a hybrid type of similarity measure. First, the text entailed by the document, such as the resolution of temporal or geographical references, is performed. Second, similarity itself is computed using a linear combination of text-based and knowledge-based similarities. The former are encoded by cosine-similarity of TF-IDF vectors (of the documents or their translations), and the latter by the overlap (as measured by Jaccard coefficient of entities that the two documents either mention directly, or are linked in the LKG to mentioned ones. The overlaps are weighted depending on how far away in the LKG the entities mentioned in the document are, and the weight coefficients are determined, along with the coefficients of the linear combination, by training a linear regression classifier (Bär et al., 2012). This approach allows us to detect similarity between documents even if they have only few entities in common, by considering the knowledge about these entities. Additionally, by comparing mentions of entities instead of their surface forms, the multilingual nature of the LKG is exploited. The knowledge-based component of the similarity computation is language agnostic, while the text-based depends only on basic NLP tools (e. g., stemming, stop-word removal) which are available for English, German, Spanish and Dutch, among others. In order to compare documents in two different languages, machine translation between them, or to a third language must be available. The semantic similarity service is a prototype, requiring further testing and refining.

3.13 Question Answering

The Question Answering (QA) service accepts a natural language question and responds with an answer, extracted from a document in a given corpus. The end-to-end system consists of three components: 1) The Query Formulation module transforms a question into a query, which can be expanded using a domain specific vocabulary from the LKG. The query is then processed through an indexer to obtain matching documents from the corresponding corpora. 2) The Answer Generation module extracts potential answers from the retrieved documents from the LKG. 3) The Answer Selection module identifies the best answer based on various criteria such as local structure of the text and global interaction between each pair of words based on specific layers of the model. The QA service is the central component of two of our use cases. In these, a user asks a natural language question along with additional information such as an appropriate jurisdiction. The question is meant to trigger a query on a set of documents related to the specific jurisdiction. These additional parameters influence the search in the Answer Selection module by determining which subset of the documents should be used. With the help of the Machine Translation service, the QA service is able to return answers in languages different from the documents' language. The benefit from the service would be the time reduction in search for a relevant article in the legislation. For a question such as "How long is paternity leave?", the system returns relevant paragraphs and articles from the Labor Law that can be further processed by the lawyer. The QA service works for English and can be retrained and adopted to other languages.

4 Orchestration of Individual Services

Our technology platform is based on microservices, which provide multiple advantages, especially in a collaborative project with a distributed set of partners from academia and industry, including use case partners. Microservices are small and autonomous and can be developed more efficiently than a monolithic, integrated system. In addition, the development and deployment of microservices can, to a very large extent, be automated, also facilitating the monitoring of individual services. A crucial advantage is concerned with the scalability of systems based on microservices, which is a lot easier than scaling monolithic systems. The communication between different services is executed over HTTP, the interfaces are documented using the OpenAPI specification. For the deployment of the containerised microservices we use Open-Shift; alternative technologies such as, among others, Kubernetes, could also be used.

In our project we conceptualise the specific requirements of the different use cases as content curation workflows (Schneider and Rehm, 2018b; Bourgonje et al., 2016a,b; Rehm et al., 2018). Workflows are defined as the execution of specific services to perform the processing of one or more documents under the umbrella of a certain task or use case. The specification of a workflow includes its input and output as well as the functionality it is supposed to perform: annotate or enrich a document, add a document to the knowledge base, search for information, etc. The project offers compliance-related features and functionalities through common services and data sets included in the LKG. Workflows make use of these services to implement the required functionality. The content curation workflows for the different use cases that we prototypically implement in the project have been defined as follows. We performed a systematic analysis of the microservices, developed in parallel, and matched them with the required functionalities for each use case. First, we determine the principal elements involved in each use case, i. e., the services, input and output. Second, we define the order in which the services have to be executed. Third, we identify the shared components in the different workflows. Currently we have defined five different workflows. Two are defined for the acquisition and population of the LKG with new information, the other three are defined to address the requirements of each use case (see Figures 1 to 3 in the appendix). We currently work with two alternative workflow management implementations that take care of the orchestration of services. The first one is based on Camunda BPM,[12] including a logic layer that manages the various processes (including NIF annotations). The second approach is based on RabbitMQ,[13] an open-source message broker, on top of which we developed our own solution for parallelising processing steps and improving the performance of the overall orchestration. In both cases, the main concept of the service orchestration is focused on the use of queuing systems, so that most of the processes could be executed in parallel and either synchronous or asynchronously.

---

[12]https://camunda.com
[13]https://www.rabbitmq.com

5   Related Work

There are several systems, platforms and approaches that are related to the technology platform, which is under development in the project LYNX. In the wider area of legal document processing, technologies from several fields are relevant, among others, knowledge technologies, citation analysis, argument mining, reasoning and information retrieval. A literature overview can be found in (Schneider and Rehm, 2018a) and (Agnoloni and Venturi, 2018).

Commercial Systems and Services – The LexisNexis[14] system is the market leader in the legal domain; it offers services, such as legal research, practical guidance, company research and media-monitoring as well as compliance and due diligence. WestLaw is an online service that allows legal professionals to find and consult relevant legal information.[15] One of its goals is to enable professionals to put together a strong argument. There are also smaller companies that offer legal research solutions and analytic environments, such as RavelLax,[16] or Lereto[17]. A commercial search engine for legal documents, iSearch, is a service offered by LegitQuest.[18] The Casetext CARA Research Suite allows uploading a brief and then retrieving, based on its contents, useful case law.[19] There is also a growing number of startup companies active in the legal domain.

Research Prototypes – Most of the documented research prototypes were developed in the 1990s under the umbrella of Computer Assisted Legal Research (CALR) (Span, 1994). In the following we briefly review several of these systems, which usually focus on one very specific feature or functionality. One example is the open source software for the analysis and visualisation of networks of Dutch case law (van Kuppevelt and van Dijck, 2017). This technology determines relevant precedents (analysing the citation network of case law), compares them with those identified in the literature, and determines clusters of related cases. A similar prototype is described by (Agnoloni et al., 2017). (Gifford, 2017) propose a search engine for legal documents where argu-

ments are extracted from appellate cases and are accessible either through selecting nodes in a litigation issue ontology or through relational keyword search. Lucem (Bhullar et al., 2016) is a system that tries to mirror the way lawyers approach legal research, developing visualisations that provide lawyers with an additional tool to approach their research results. Eunomos is a prototype that semi-automates the construction and analysis of knowledge (Boella et al., 2012).

6   Summary and Future Work

This article presents the technology platform currently under development in the project LYNX, focusing upon processing services. These serve two main purposes: 1) to extract semantic information from a large and heterogeneous set of documents to ingest the extracted information into the Legal Knowledge Graph; 2) to extract semantic information from documents that users of the platform work with. In addition to the semantic extraction of information and knowledge, we provide services for the processing and curation of whole documents (summarisation, translation) with the goal of mapping extracted terms and concepts to the LKG, and services that aim at accessing the LKG (question answering). We currently experiment with two different curation workflow managers to make specific sets of services available for specific use cases. Future work includes completing development work on the services, adapting the services to all languages required in the project's use cases, implementing the prototype applications and developing the freely accessible web interface of the platform.

Acknowledgments

This work has been partially funded by the project LYNX, which has received funding from the European Union's Horizon 2020 research and innovation programme under grant agreement no. 780602. For more information please see `http://www.lynx-project.eu`.

References

Tommaso Agnoloni, Lorenzo Bacci, Ginevra Peruginelli, Marc van Opijnen, Jos van den Oever, Monica Palmirani, Luca Cervone, Octavian Bujor, Arantxa Arsuaga Lecuona, Alberto Boada García, Luigi Di Caro, and Giovanni Siragusa. 2017. Linking european case law: BO-ECLI parser, an open

---

[14]`https://www.lexisnexis.com`
[15]`http://legalsolutions.thomsonreuters.com/law-products/westlaw-legal-research/`
[16]`http://ravellaw.com`
[17]`https://www.lereto.at`
[18]`https://www.legitquest.com`
[19]`https://casetext.com`

framework for the automatic extraction of legal links. In (Wyner and Casini, 2017), pages 113–118.

Tommaso Agnoloni and Giulia Venturi. 2018. Semantic processing of legal texts. In Jacqueline Visconti, editor, *Handbook of Communication in the Legal Sphere*, pages 109–138. De Gruyter, Berlin, Boston.

Mehdi Allahyari, Seyedamin Pouriyeh, Mehdi Assefi, Sacid Safaci, Elizabcth D Trippc, Juan B Guticrrez, and Krys Kochut. 2017. Text Summarization Techniques: A brief Survey. *arXiv preprint arXiv:1707.02268.*

Daniel Bär, Chris Biemann, Iryna Gurevych, and Torsten Zesch. 2012. Ukp: Computing semantic textual similarity by combining multiple content similarity measures. In *Proceedings of the First Joint Conference on Lexical and Computational Semantics-Volume 1: Proceedings of the main conference and the shared task, and Volume 2: Proceedings of the Sixth International Workshop on Semantic Evaluation*, pages 435–440. Association for Computational Linguistics.

Darina Benikova, Chris Biemann, Max Kisselew, and Sebastian Pad. 2014. GermEval 2014 Named Entity Recognition Shared Task: Companion Paper. In *Proceedings of the KONVENS GermEval workshop*, pages 104–112, Hildesheim, Germany.

Darina Benikova, Seid Muhie Yimam, Prabhakaran Santhanam, and Chris Biemann. 2015. Germaner: Free open german named entity recognition tool. In *Proceedings of the International Conference of the German Society for Computational Linguistics and Language Technology, GSCL 2015, University of Duisburg-Essen, Germany, 30th September - 2nd October 2015*, pages 31–38.

Jagjoth Bhullar, Nathan Lam, Kenneth Pham, Adithya Prabhakaran, and Albert Joseph Santillano. 2016. *Lucem: A Legal Research Tool*, 63. Computer Engineering Senior Theses.

G. Boella, L. di Caro, L. Humphreys, L. Robaldo, and L. van der Torre. 2012. Nlp challenges for eunomos, a tool to build and manage legal knowledge.

Peter Bourgonje, Julian Moreno-Schneider, Jan Nehring, Georg Rehm, Felix Sasaki, and Ankit Srivastava. 2016a. Towards a Platform for Curation Technologies: Enriching Text Collections with a Semantic-Web Layer. In *The Semantic Web*, number 9989 in Lecture Notes in Computer Science, pages 65–68. Springer. ESWC 2016 Satellite Events. Heraklion, Crete, Greece, May 29 – June 2, 2016 Revised Selected Papers.

Peter Bourgonje, Julián Moreno Schneider, Georg Rehm, and Felix Sasaki. 2016b. Processing Document Collections to Automatically Extract Linked Data: Semantic Storytelling Technologies for Smart Curation Workflows. In *Proceedings of the 2nd International Workshop on Natural Language Generation and the Semantic Web (WebNLG 2016)*, pages

13–16, Edinburgh, UK. The Association for Computational Linguistics.

Manaal Faruqui and Sebastian Padó. 2010. Training and evaluating a german named entity recognizer with semantic generalization. In *Semantic Approaches in Natural Language Processing: Proceedings of the 10th Conference on Natural Language Processing, KONVENS 2010, September 6-8, 2010, Saarland University, Saarbrücken, Germany*, pages 129–133. universaar, Universitätsverlag des Saarlandes / Saarland University Press / Presses universitaires de la Sarre.

Jenny Rose Finkel, Trond Grenager, and Christopher D. Manning. 2005. Incorporating non-local information into information extraction systems by gibbs sampling. In *ACL 2005, 43rd Annual Meeting of the Association for Computational Linguistics, Proceedings of the Conference, 25-30 June 2005, University of Michigan, USA*, pages 363–370. The Association for Computer Linguistics.

Demian Gholipour Ghalandari. 2017. Revisiting the Centroid-based Method: A Strong Baseline for Multi-Document Summarization. *arXiv preprint arXiv:1708.07690.*

Matthew Gifford. 2017. Lexridelaw: an argument based legal search engine. In *ICAIL '17*.

Wael H Gomaa and Aly A Fahmy. 2013. A survey of text similarity approaches. *International Journal of Computer Applications*, 68(13):13–18.

Sebastian Hellmann, Jens Lehmann, Sören Auer, and Martin Brümmer. 2013. Integrating NLP using Linked Data. In *12th International Semantic Web Conference*. 21-25 October.

Zhiheng Huang, Wei Xu, and Kai Yu. 2015. Bidirectional LSTM-CRF models for sequence tagging. *CoRR*, abs/1508.01991.

Marcin Junczys-Dowmunt, Roman Grundkiewicz, Tomasz Dwojak, Hieu Hoang, Kenneth Heafield, Tom Neckermann, Frank Seide, Ulrich Germann, Alham Fikri Aji, Nikolay Bogoychev, André F T Martins, and Alexandra Birch. 2018. Marian: Fast Neural Machine Translation in C++. *arXiv preprint arXiv:1804.00344.*

Dafne van Kuppevelt and Gijs van Dijck. 2017. Answering legal research questions about dutch case law with network analysis and visualization. In (Wyner and Casini, 2017), pages 95–100.

Guillaume Lample, Miguel Ballesteros, Sandeep Subramanian, Kazuya Kawakami, and Chris Dyer. 2016. Neural architectures for named entity recognition. In *NAACL HLT 2016, The 2016 Conference of the North American Chapter of the Association for Computational Linguistics: Human Language Technologies, San Diego California, USA, June 12-17, 2016*, pages 260–270.

Tomas Mikolov, Ilya Sutskever, Kai Chen, Greg S Corrado, and Jeff Dean. 2013. Distributed Representations of Words and Phrases and their Compositionality. In *Advances in neural information processing systems*, pages 3111–3119.

Joel Larocca Neto, Alexandre D Santos, Celso AA Kaestner, Neto Alexandre, D Santos, et al. 2000. Document Clustering and Text Summarization.

Kishore Papineni, Salim Roukos, Todd Ward, and Wei-Jing Zhu. 2002. BLEU: a Method for Automatic Evaluation of Machine Translation. In *Proceedings of the 40th annual meeting on association for computational linguistics*, pages 311–318. Association for Computational Linguistics.

Jeffrey Pennington, Richard Socher, and Christopher Manning. 2014. Glove: Global Vectors for Word Representation. In *Proceedings of the 2014 conference on empirical methods in natural language processing (EMNLP)*, pages 1532–1543.

Mārcis Pinnis, Nikola Ljubešić, Dan Ştefănescu, Inguna Skadiņa, Marko Tadić, and Tatiana Gornostay. 2012. Term Extraction, Tagging, and Mapping Tools for Under-Resourced Languages. In *Proceedings of the 10th Conference on Terminology and Knowledge Engineering (TKE 2012)*, June 2012, pages 193–208, Madrid, Spain.

Georg Rehm, Julián Moreno Schneider, Peter Bourgonje, Ankit Srivastava, Rolf Fricke, Jan Thomsen, Jing He, Joachim Quantz, Armin Berger, Luca König, Sören Räuchle, Jens Gerth, and David Wabnitz. 2018. Different Types of Automated and Semi-Automated Semantic Storytelling: Curation Technologies for Different Sectors. In *Language Technologies for the Challenges of the Digital Age: 27th International Conference, GSCL 2017, Berlin, Germany, September 13-14, 2017, Proceedings*, number 10713 in Lecture Notes in Artificial Intelligence (LNAI), pages 232–247, Cham, Switzerland. Gesellschaft für Sprachtechnologie und Computerlinguistik e.V., Springer. 13/14 September 2017.

Nils Reimers and Iryna Gurevych. 2017. Reporting score distributions makes a difference: Performance study of lstm-networks for sequence tagging. In *Proceedings of the 2017 Conference on Empirical Methods in Natural Language Processing*, pages 338–348. Association for Computational Linguistics.

Xiang Ren, Zeqiu Wu, Wenqi He, Meng Qu, Clare R Voss, Heng Ji, Tarek F Abdelzaher, and Jiawei Han. 2017. Cotype: Joint extraction of typed entities and relations with knowledge bases. In *Proceedings of the 26th International Conference on World Wide Web*, pages 1015–1024. International World Wide Web Conferences Steering Committee.

Artem Revenko and Víctor Mireles. 2017. Discrimination of word senses with hypernyms. In *Proceedings of the 5th International Workshop on Linked Data for Information Extraction co-located with the 16th International Semantic Web Conference (ISWC 2017), Vienna, Austria, October 22, 2017.*, volume 1946 of *CEUR Workshop Proceedings*, pages 50–61. CEUR-WS.org.

Martin Riedl and Sebastian Padó. 2018. A named entity recognition shootout for german. In *Proceedings of the 56th Annual Meeting of the Association for Computational Linguistics (Volume 2: Short Papers)*, volume 2, pages 120–125. Association for Computational Linguistics.

Gaetano Rossiello, Pierpaolo Basile, and Giovanni Semeraro. 2017. Centroid-based Text Summarization through Compositionality of Word Embeddings. In *Proceedings of the MultiLing 2017 Workshop on Summarization and Summary Evaluation Across Source Types and Genres*, pages 12–21.

Julian Moreno Schneider and Georg Rehm. 2018a. Curation Technologies for the Construction and Utilisation of Legal Knowledge Graphs. In *Proceedings of the LREC 2018 Workshop on Language Resources and Technologies for the Legal Knowledge Graph*, pages 23–29, Miyazaki, Japan. 12 May 2018.

Julian Moreno Schneider and Georg Rehm. 2018b. Towards a Workflow Manager for Curation Technologies in the Legal Domain. In *Proceedings of the LREC 2018 Workshop on Language Resources and Technologies for the Legal Knowledge Graph*, pages 30–35, Miyazaki, Japan. 12 May 2018.

Georges Span. 1994. Lites: An intelligent tutoring system shell for legal education. *International Review of Law, Computers & Technology*, 8(1):103–113.

Karen Spärck Jones. 1972. A Statistical Interpretation of Term Specificity and Its Application in Retrieval. *Journal of Documentation*, 28:11—-21.

Jannik Strötgen and Michael Gertz. 2010. HeidelTime: High Quality Rule-based Extraction and Normalization of Temporal Expressions. In *Proceedings of the 5th International Workshop on Semantic Evaluation*, SemEval '10, pages 321–324, Stroudsburg, PA, USA. Association for Computational Linguistics.

Adam Z. Wyner and Giovanni Casini, editors. 2017. *Legal Knowledge and Information Systems - JURIX 2017: The Thirtieth Annual Conference, Luxembourg, 13-15 December 2017*, volume 302 of *Frontiers in Artificial Intelligence and Applications*. IOS Press.

A Appendix: Examples of Use-Case-specific Curation Workflows

The following three figures are additional material with regard to Section 4. They provide illustrative examples of use-case-specific processing service and curation workflows.

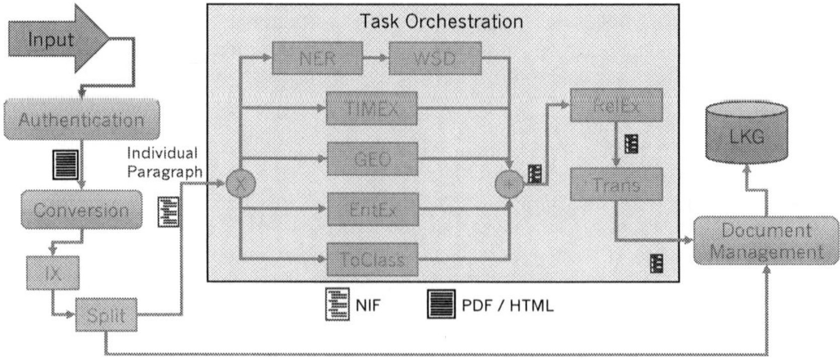

Figure 1: Legal Knowledge Graph population workflow

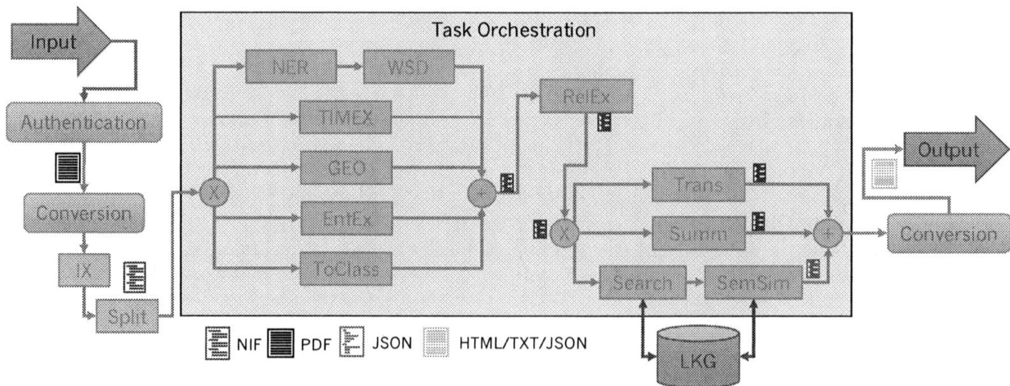

Figure 2: Workflow of the Contract Analysis use case

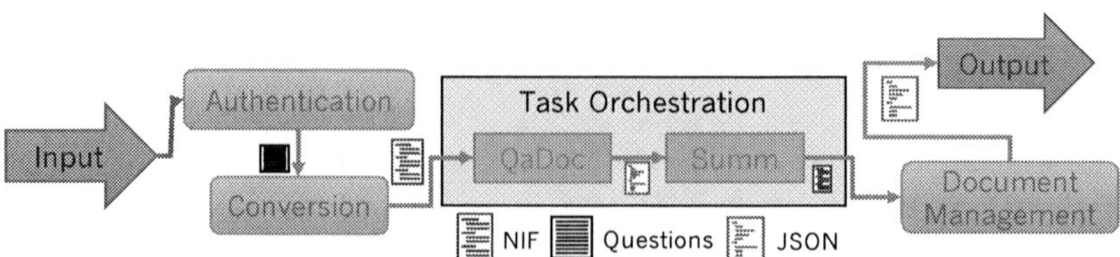

Figure 3: Workflow of the Labour Law use case

Legal Area Classification: A Comparative Study of Text Classifiers on Singapore Supreme Court Judgments

Jerrold Soh Tsin Howe[*], **Lim How Khang**, and **Ian Ernst Chai**[**]

[*]Singapore Management University, School of Law
[**]Attorney-General's Chambers, Singapore
jerroldsoh@smu.edu.sg, howkhang.lim@gmail.com
ian_ernst_chai@agc.gov.sg

Abstract

This paper conducts a comparative study on the performance of various machine learning ("ML") approaches for classifying judgments into legal areas. Using a novel dataset of 6,227 Singapore Supreme Court judgments, we investigate how state-of-the-art NLP methods compare against traditional statistical models when applied to a legal corpus that comprised few but lengthy documents. All approaches tested, including topic model, word embedding, and language model-based classifiers, performed well with as little as a few hundred judgments. However, more work needs to be done to optimize state-of-the-art methods for the legal domain.

1 Introduction

Every legal case falls into one or more areas of law ("legal areas"). These areas are lawyers' shorthand for the subset of legal principles and rules governing the case. Thus lawyers often triage a new case by asking if it falls within tort, contract, or other legal areas. Answering this allows unresolved cases to be funneled to the right experts and for resolved precedents to be efficiently retrieved. Legal database providers routinely provide area-based search functionality; courts often publish judgments labelled by legal area.

The law therefore yields pockets of expert-labelled text. A system that classifies legal texts by area would be useful for enriching older, typically unlabelled judgments with metadata for more efficient search and retrieval. The system can also suggest areas for further inquiry by predicting which areas a new text falls within.

Despite its potential, this problem, which we refer to and later define as "legal area classification", remains relatively unexplored. One explanation is the relative scarcity of labelled documents in the law (typically in the low thousands), at least by

deep learning standards. This problem is acute in smaller jurisdictions like Singapore, where the number of labelled cases is limited by the few cases that actually reach the courts. Another explanation is that legal texts are typically longer than the customer reviews, tweets, and other documents typical in NLP research.

Against this backdrop, this paper uses a novel dataset of Singapore Supreme Court judgments to comparatively study the performance of various text classification approaches for legal area classification. Our specific research question is as follows: how do recent state-of-the-art models compare against traditional statistical models when applied to legal corpora that, typically, comprise few but lengthy documents?

We find that there are challenges when it comes to adapting state-of-the-art deep learning classifiers for tasks in the legal domain. Traditional topic models still outperform the more recent neural-based classifiers on certain metrics, suggesting that emerging research (fit specially to tasks with numerous short documents) may not carry well into the legal domain unless more work is done to optimize them for legal NLP tasks. However, that shallow models perform well suggests that enough exploitable information exists in legal texts for deep learning approaches better-tailored to the legal domain to perform as well if not better.

2 Related Work

Papers closest to ours are those that likewise examine legal area classification. Goncalves and Quaresma (2005) used bag-of-words ("BOW") features learned using TF-IDF to train linear support vector machines ("linSVMs") to classify decisions of the Portuguese Attorney General's Office into 10 legal areas. Boella et al. (2012) used

Proceedings of the Natural Legal Language Processing Workshop 2019, pages 67–77
Minneapolis, Minesotta, June 7, 2019. ©2019 Association for Computational Linguistics

TF-IDF features enriched by a semi-automatically linked legal ontology and linSVMs to classify Italian legislation into 15 civil law areas. Sulea et al. (2017) classified French Supreme Court judgments into 8 civil law areas, again using BOW features learned using Latent Semantic Analysis ("LSA") (Deerwester et al., 1990) and linSVMs.

On legal text classification more generally, Aletras et al. (2016); Liu and Chen (2017); Sulea et al. (2017) used BOW features extracted from judgments and linSVMs for predicting case outcomes. Talley and O'Kane (2012) use BOW features and a linSVM to classify contract clauses.

NLP has also been used for legal information extraction. Venkatesh (2013) used Latent Dirichlet Allocation (Blei et al., 2003) ("LDA") to cluster Indian court judgments. Falakmasir and Ashley (2017) used vector space models to extract legal factors motivating case outcomes from American trade secret misappropriation judgments.

There is also growing scholarship on legal text analysis. Typically, topic models are used to extract N-gram clusters from legal corpora, such as Constitutions, statutes, and Parliamentary records, then assessed for legal significance (Young, 2013; Carter et al., 2016). More recently, Ash and Chen (2019) used document embeddings trained on United States Supreme Court judgments to encode and study spatial and temporal patterns across federal judges and appellate courts.

We contribute to this literature by (1) benchmarking new text classification techniques against legal area classification, and (2) more deeply exploring how document scarcity and length affect performance. Beyond BOW features and linSVMs, we use word embeddings and newly-developed language models. Our novel label set comprises 31 legal areas relevant to Singapore's *common* law system. Judgments of the Singapore Supreme Court have thus far not been exploited. We also draw an important but overlooked distinction between *cases* and *judgments*.

3   Problem Description

Legal areas generally refer to a subset of related legal principles and rules governing certain dispute types. There is no universal set of legal areas. Areas like tort and equity, well-known in English and American law, have no direct analogue in certain civil law systems. Societal change may create new areas of law like data protection. However, the set of legal areas in a given jurisdiction and time is well-defined. Denote this as L.

Lawyers typically attribute a given case c_i to a given legal area $l \in L$ if c_i's attributes v_{c_i} (*e.g.* a vector of its facts, parties involved, and procedural trail) raise legal issues that implicate some principle or rule in l. Cases may fall into more than one legal area but never none.

Cases should be distinguished from the *judgments* courts write when resolving them (denoted j_{c_i}). j_{c_i} may not state everything in v_{c_i} because judges need only discuss issues material to how the case should be resolved. Suppose a claimant mounts two claims on the same issue against a defendant in tort, and in trademark law. If the judge finds for the claimant in tort, he/she may not discuss trademark at all (though some may still do so). Thus, even though v_{c_i} raises trademark issues, j_{c_i} may not contain any N-grams discussing the same. It is possible that a v_{c_i} we would assign to l leads to a j_{c_i} we would not assign to l. The upshot is that judgments are incomplete sources of case information; classifying *judgments* is not the same as classifying *cases*.

This paper focuses on the former. We treat this as a supervised legal text multi-class and multi-label classification task. The goal is to learn f^* : $j_i \mapsto L_{j_i}$ where $*$ denotes optimality.

4   Data

The corpus comprises 6,227 judgments of the Singapore Supreme Court written in English.[1] Each judgment comes in PDF format, with its legal areas labelled by the Court. The median judgment has 6,968 tokens and is significantly longer than the typical customer review or news article commonly found in datasets for benchmarking machine learning models on text classification.

The raw dataset yielded 51 different legal area labels. Some labels were subsets of larger legal areas and were manually merged into those. Label imbalance was present in the dataset so we limited the label set to the 30 most frequent areas. Remaining labels (252 in total) were then mapped to the label "others". Table 1 shows the final label distribution, truncated for brevity. Appendix A.2 presents the full label distribution and all label merging decisions.

---

[1]The judgments were issued between 3 January 2000 and 18 February 2019 and were downloaded from `http://www.singaporelawwatch.sg`, an official repository of Singapore Supreme Court judgments.

Label	Count
civil_procedure	1369
contract_law	861
criminal_procedure_and_sentencing	775
criminal_law	734
family_law	491
...	...
others	252
...	...
banking_law	75
restitution	60
agency_law	57
res_judicata	49
insurance_law	39
Total	**8853**

Table 1: Truncated Distribution of Final Labels

5 Models and Methods

Given label imbalance, we held out 10% of the corpus by stratified iterative sampling (Sechidis et al., 2011; Szymaski and Kajdanowicz, 2017). For each model type, we trained three separate classifiers on *the same* 10% (n=588), 50% (n=2795), and 100% (n=5599) of the remaining *training* set ("training subsets"), again split by stratified iteration, and tested them against *the same* 10% holdout. We studied four model types of increasing sophistication and recency. These are briefly explained here. Further implementation details may be found in the Appendix A.3.

5.1 Baseline Models

$base_{pdf}$ is a dummy classifier which predicts 1 for any label which expectation equals or exceeds $1/31$ (the total number of labels).

$count_m$ uses a keyword matching strategy that emulates how lawyers may approach the task. It predicts 1 for any label if its associated terms appear $\geq m$ non-unique times in j_i. m is a manually-set threshold. A label's set of associated terms is the union of (a) the set of its sub-labels in the training subset, and (b) the set of non-stopword unigrams in the label itself. We manually added potentially problematic unigrams like "law" to the stopwords list. Suppose the label "tort_law" appears twice in the training subset, first with sub-label "negligence", and later with sub-label "harassment". The associated terms set would be $\{tort, negligence, harassment\}$.

5.2 Topic Models

lsa_k is a one-vs-rest linSVM trained using k topics extracted by LSA. We used LSA and linSVMs as benchmarks because, despite their vintage, they remain a staple of the *legal* text classification literature (see Section 2 above). Indeed, LDA models were also tested but strictly underperformed LSA models in all experiment and were thus not reported. Feature vectorizers and classifiers from scikit-learn (Pedregosa et al., 2011) were retrained for each training subset with all default settings except sublinear term frequencies were used in the TF-IDF step as recommended by Scikit-Learn (2017).

5.3 Word Embedding Feature Models

Word vectors pre-trained on large corpora have been shown to capture syntactic and semantic word properties (Mikolov et al., 2013; Pennington et al., 2014). We leverage on this by initializing word vectors using pre-trained GloVe vectors of length 300.[2] Judgment vectors were then composed in three ways: $glove_{avg}$ average-pools each word vector in j_i (i.e. average-pooling); $glove_{max}$ uses max-pooling (Shen et al., 2018); $glove_{cnn}$ feeds the word vectors through a shallow convolutional neural network ("CNN") (Kim, 2014). We chose to implement a shallow CNN model for $glove_{cnn}$ because it has been shown that deep CNN models do not necessarily perform better on text classification tasks (Le et al., 2018). To derive label predictions, judgment vectors were then fed through a multi-layer perceptron followed by a sigmoid function.

5.4 Pre-trained Language Models

Recent work has also shown that language representation models pre-trained on large unlabelled corpora and fine-tuned onto specific tasks significantly outperform models trained only on task-specific data. This method of transfer learning is particularly useful in legal NLP, given the lack of labelled data in the legal domain. We thus evaluated Devlin et al. (2018)'s state-of-the-art BERT model using published pre-trained weights from $bert_{base}$ (12-layers; 110M parameters) and $bert_{large}$ (24-layers; 340M parameters).[3] However, as BERT's self-attention transformer archi-

---

[2] http://nlp.stanford.edu/data/glove.6B.zip

[3] https://github.com/google-research/bert

tecture (Vaswani et al., 2017) only accepts up to 512 Wordpiece tokens (Wu et al., 2016) as input, we used only the first 512 tokens of each j_i to fine-tune both models.[4] We considered splitting the judgment into shorter segments and passing each segment through the BERT model but doing so would require extensive modification to the original fine-tuning method; hence we left this for future experimentation. In this light, we also benchmarked Howard and Ruder (2018)'s ULM-FiT model which accepts longer inputs due to its stacked-LSTM architecture.

6 Results

Given our multi-label setting, we evaluated the models on and report micro- and macro-averaged F1 scores (Table 2), precision (Table 3), and recall (Table 4). Micro-averaging calculates the metric globally while macro-averaging first calculates the metric *within each label* before averaging across labels. Thus, micro-averaged metrics equally-weight each *sample* and better indicate a model's performance on common labels whereas macro-averaged metrics equally-weight each *label* and better indicate performance on rare labels.

6.1 F1 Score

Subset	10%	50%	100%
$bert_{large}$	45.1 [57.9]	56.7 [63.8]	60.7 [66.3]
$bert_{base}$	43.1 [53.6]	52.0 [57.6]	56.2 [63.9]
$ulmfit$	**45.7** [62.8]	45.9 [63.0]	49.2 [64.3]
$glove_{cnn}$	40.7 [62.2]	58.7 [67.1]	63.1 [70.8]
$glove_{avg}$	36.7 [49.7]	**59.1** [64.3]	61.5 [65.6]
$glove_{max}$	29.2 [47.4]	47.8 [59.9]	52.5 [63.2]
lsa_{250}	37.9 [**63.5**]	55.2 [**70.8**]	**63.2** [**73.3**]
lsa_{100}	30.6 [58.5]	51.8 [68.5]	57.1 [70.8]
$count_{25}$	32.6 [36.1]	31.8 [30.6]	27.7 [28.1]
$base_{pdf}$	5.2 [17.3]	5.5 [16.6]	5.5 [16.6]

Table 2: Macro [Micro] F1 Scores Across Experiments

Across the three data subsets, all ML models consistently outperformed the statistical and keyword-matching baselines $base_{pdf}$ and $count_{25}$ respectively. Notably, even with limited training data (in the 10% subset), most ML approaches surpassed $count_{25}$ which, to recall, emulates how lawyers may use keyword searches for

legal area classification. Deep transfer learning approaches in particular performed well in this data-constrained setting, with $bert_{large}$, $bert_{base}$, and $ulmfit$ producing the best three macro-F1s. $ulmfit$ also achieved the second best micro-F1.

As more training data became available at the 50% and 100% subsets, the ML classifiers' advantage over the baseline models widened to around 30 percentage points on average. Word-embedding models in particular showed significant improvements. $glove_{avg}$ and $glove_{cnn}$ outperformed most of the other models (with F1 scores of 63.1 and 61.5 respectively). Within the embedding models, $glove_{cnn}$ generally outperformed $glove_{avg}$ while $glove_{max}$ performed significantly worse than both and thus appears to be an unsuitable pooling strategy for this task.

Most surprisingly, lsa_{250} emerged as the best performing model on both micro- and macro-averaged F1 scores for the 100% subset. The model also produced the highest micro-averaged F1 score across all three data subsets, suggesting that common labels were handled well. lsa_{250}'s strong performance was fuelled primarily by high *precision* rather than recall, as discussed below.

6.2 Precision

Subset	10%	50%	100%
$bert_{large}$	54.7 [65.8]	57.1 [59.7]	63.6 [64.3]
$bert_{base}$	41.4 [45.1]	48.1 [50.0]	61.4 [67.2]
$ulmfit$	49.3 [63.7]	46.6 [61.4]	48.7 [63.2]
$glove_{cnn}$	50.7 [69.8]	63.4 [68.5]	66.7 [72.9]
$glove_{avg}$	**62.5** [68.0]	67.0 [68.1]	64.8 [68.2]
$glove_{max}$	51.3 [65.1]	47.3 [56.6]	59.2 [68.6]
lsa_{250}	56.7 [76.1]	70.0 [81.1]	**83.4** [81.7]
lsa_{100}	52.3 [**77.2**]	**73.8** [**81.9**]	73.9 [**83.7**]
$count_{25}$	30.2 [26.4]	26.4 [19.8]	23.0 [17.8]
$base_{pdf}$	2.9 [10.0]	3.1 [9.5]	3.1 [9.5]

Table 3: Macro [Micro] Precision Across Experiments

As with F1 score, ML models outperformed baselines by large margins on precision. LSA models performed remarkably well here: except in the 10% subset, where $glove_{cnn}$ recorded the highest macro-precision, top results for both precision measures belonged to either lsa_{100} or lsa_{250}. Notably, on the 100% subset, lsa_{250} managed over 80% on micro- and macro-precision.

---

[4]Alternative strategies for selecting the 512 tokens trialed performed consistently worse and are not reported.

Subset	10%	50%	100%
$bert_{large}$	43.2 [51.7]	**59.0 [68.5]**	61.6 [68.5]
$bert_{base}$	**50.0 [66.1]**	58.7 [67.9]	54.2 [60.9]
$ulmfit$	46.1 [61.8]	48.4 [64.8]	52.6 [65.4]
$glove_{cnn}$	37.4 [56.0]	58.2 [65.8]	**62.3 [68.8]**
$glove_{avg}$	28.7 [39.2]	56.5 [60.9]	62.1 [63.1]
$glove_{max}$	23.2 [37.2]	49.9 [63.6]	49.0 [58.5]
lsa_{250}	32.7 [54.4]	50.2 [62.8]	57.8 [66.5]
lsa_{100}	25.7 [47.0]	45.3 [58.9]	51.6 [61.4]
$count_{25}$	48.1 [56.9]	57.5 [66.3]	59.9 [66.9]
$base_{pdf}$	29.0 [64.5]	32.3 [67.7]	32.3 [67.7]

Table 4: Macro [Micro] Recall Across Experiments

6.3 Recall

LSA's impressive results, however, stop short at recall. A striking observation from Table 4 is that LSA and most other ML models did *worse* than $count_{25}$ on *both* micro- and macro-recall *across all data subsets*. Thus, a keyword-search strategy seems to be a simple yet strong baseline for identifying and retrieving judgments by legal area, particularly when recall is paramount and an ontology of area-related terms is available. To some extent this reflects realities in legal practice, where false negatives (missing relevant precedents) have greater potential to undermine legal argument than false positives (discovering irrelevant precedents).

Instead of LSA, the strongest performers here were the BERT models which produced the best micro- and macro-recall on the 10% and 50% subsets and $glove_{cnn}$ for the 100% training subset.

7 Discussion

We initially expected pre-trained language models, being the state-of-the-art on many non-legal NLP tasks, to perform best here as well. That an LSA-based linSVM would outperform both word-embedding and language models by many measures surprised us. How LSA achieved this is explored in Appendix A.4 which presents a sample of the (quite informative) topics extracted.

One caveat to interpreting our results: we focused on comparing the models' *out-of-box* performance, rather than comparing the models at their best (i.e. after extensive cross-validation and tuning). Specifically, the BERT models' inability to be fine-tuned on longer input texts meant that they competed at a disadvantage, having been shown only selected judgment portions. Despite this, BERT models proved competitive on smaller training subsets. Likewise, while $ulmfit$ performed well on the 10% subset (suggesting that it benefited from encoder pre-training), the model struggled to leverage additional training data and recorded only modest improvements on the larger training subsets.

Thus, our answer to the research question stated in Section 1 is a nuanced one: while state-of-the-art models do not clearly outperform traditional statistical models when applied *out-of-box* to legal corpora, they show promise for dealing with data constraints particularly if further adapted and fine-tuned to accommodate longer texts. This should inform future research.

8 Conclusion and Future Work

This paper comparatively benchmarked traditional topic models against more recent, sophisticated, and computationally intensive techniques on the legal area classification task. We found that while data scarcity affects all ML classifiers, certain classifiers, especially pre-trained language models, could perform well with as few as 588 labelled judgments.

Our results also suggest that more work can be done to adapt state-of-the-art NLP models for the legal domain. Two areas seem promising: (1) creating *law-specific* datasets and baselines for training and benchmarking legal text classifiers, and (2) exploring representation learning techniques that leverage transfer learning methods but scale well on long texts. For the latter, possible directions here include exploring different CNN architectures and their hyperparameters, using contextualized word embeddings, and using feature extraction methods on pre-trained language models like BERT (as opposed to fine-tuning them) so that they can be used on longer text inputs. As Lord Denning said in *Packer v Packer* [1953] EWCA Civ J0511-3:

> "If we never do anything which has not been done before, we shall never get anywhere. The law will stand whilst the rest of the world goes on; and that will be bad for both."

Acknowledgments

We thank the anonymous reviewers for their helpful comments and the Singapore Academy of Law for permitting us to scrape and use this corpus.

References

Nikolaos Aletras, Dimitrios Tsarapatsanis, Daniel Preoiuc-Pietro, and Vasileios Lampos. 2016. Predicting judicial decisions of the european court of human rights: A natural language processing perspective. *PeerJ Computer Science*, 2.

Elliott Ash and Daniel L. Chen. 2019. Case vectors: Spatial representations of the law using document embeddings. In Michael Livermore and Daniel Rockmore, editors, *Computational Analysis of Law*. Sante Fe Institute Press. (forthcoming).

David M. Blei, Andrew Y. Ng, and Michael I. Jordan. 2003. Latent dirichlet allocation. *Journal of Machine Learning Research*, 3:993–1022.

Guido Boella, Luigi Di Caro, Llio Humphreys, and Livio Robaldo. 2012. Using legal ontology to improve classification in the eunomos legal document and knowledge management system. In *Semantic Processing of Legal Texts (SPLeT-2012) Workshop Programme*, page 13.

David J Carter, James J. Brown, and Adel Rahmani. 2016. Reading the high court at a distance: Topic modelling the legal subject matter and judicial activity of the high court of australia, 1903-2015. *University of New South Wales Law Journal*, 39(4):13001354.

Scott Deerwester, Susan T. Dumais, George W. Furnas, Thomas K. Landauer, and Richard Harshman. 1990. Indexing by latent semantic analysis. *Journal of the American Society for Information Science*, 41(6):391–407.

Jacob Devlin, Ming-Wei Chang, Kenton Lee, and Kristina Toutanova. 2018. BERT: pre-training of deep bidirectional transformers for language understanding. *CoRR*, abs/1810.04805.

Mohammad Hassan Falakmasir and Kevin Ashley. 2017. Utilizing vector space models for identifying legal factors from text. In *Legal Knowledge and Information Systems: JURIX 2017*. IOS Press.

Teresa Goncalves and Paulo Quaresma. 2005. Evaluating preprocessing techniques in a text classification problem. In *Proceedings of the Conference of the Brazilian Computer Society*.

Matthew Honnibal and Ines Montani. 2017. spacy 2: Natural language understanding with bloom embeddings, convolutional neural networks and incremental parsing. *To appear.*

Jeremy Howard and Sebastian Ruder. 2018. Universal language model fine-tuning for text classification. In *Proceedings of the 56th Annual Meeting of the Association for Computational Linguistics, ACL 2018, Melbourne, Australia, July 15-20, 2018, Volume 1: Long Papers*, pages 328–339.

Yoon Kim. 2014. Convolutional neural networks for sentence classification. In *Proceedings of the 2014 Conference on Empirical Methods in Natural Language Processing (EMNLP)*, pages 1746–1751. Association for Computational Linguistics.

Hoa T. Le, Christophe Cerisara, and Alexandre Denis. 2018. Do convolutional networks need to be deep for text classification ? In *AAAI Workshops*.

Zhenyu Liu and Huanhuan Chen. 2017. A predictive performance comparison of machine learning models for judicial cases. *2017 IEEE Symposium Series on Computational Intelligence*.

Tomas Mikolov, Ilya Sutskever, Kai Chen, Greg Corrado, and Jeffrey Dean. 2013. Distributed representations of words and phrases and their compositionality. In *Proceedings of the 26th International Conference on Neural Information Processing Systems - Volume 2*, NIPS'13, pages 3111–3119, USA. Curran Associates Inc.

F. Pedregosa, G. Varoquaux, A. Gramfort, V. Michel, B. Thirion, O. Grisel, M. Blondel, P. Prettenhofer, R. Weiss, V. Dubourg, J. Vanderplas, A. Passos, D. Cournapeau, M. Brucher, M. Perrot, and E. Duchesnay. 2011. Scikit-learn: Machine learning in Python. *Journal of Machine Learning Research*, 12:2825–2830.

Jeffrey Pennington, Richard Socher, and Christopher D. Manning. 2014. Glove: Global vectors for word representation. In *Empirical Methods in Natural Language Processing (EMNLP)*, pages 1532–1543.

Scikit-Learn. 2017. *Truncated Singular Value Decomposition and Latent Semantic Analysis.* Retrieved 28 Aug 2018 at http://scikit-learn.org/stable/modules/decomposition.html#lsa.

Konstantinos Sechidis, Grigorios Tsoumakas, and Ioannis Vlahavas. 2011. On the stratification of multi-label data. *Machine Learning and Knowledge Discovery in Databases*, pages 145–158.

Dinghan Shen, Guoyin Wang, Wenlin Wang, Martin Renqiang Min, Qinliang Su, Yizhe Zhang, Chunyuan Li, Ricardo Henao, and Lawrence Carin. 2018. Baseline needs more love: On simple word-embedding-based models and associated pooling mechanisms. In *Proceedings of the 56th Annual Meeting of the Association for Computational Linguistics (Volume 1: Long Papers)*, pages 440–450. Association for Computational Linguistics.

Vikash Singh. 2017. Replace or Retrieve Keywords In Documents at Scale. *ArXiv e-prints*.

Octavia-Maria Sulea, Marcos Zampieri, Mihaela Vela, and Josef Van Genabith. 2017. Predicting the law area and decisions of french supreme court cases. *RANLP 2017 - Recent Advances in Natural Language Processing Meet Deep Learning*.

Piotr Szymaski and Tomasz Kajdanowicz. 2017. A network perspective on stratification of multi-label data. In *Proceedings of the First International Workshop on Learning with Imbalanced Domains: Theory and Applications*, volume 74 of *Proceedings of Machine Learning Research*, pages 22–35, ECML-PKDD, Skopje, Macedonia. PMLR.

Eric Talley and Drew O'Kane. 2012. The measure of a mac: A machine-learning protocol for analyzing force majeure clauses in m&a agreements. *Journal of Institutional and Theoretical Economics JITE*, 168(1):181–201.

Ashish Vaswani, Noam Shazeer, Niki Parmar, Jakob Uszkoreit, Llion Jones, Aidan N Gomez, Ł ukasz Kaiser, and Illia Polosukhin. 2017. Attention is all you need. In I. Guyon, U. V. Luxburg, S. Bengio, H. Wallach, R. Fergus, S. Vishwanathan, and R. Garnett, editors, *Advances in Neural Information Processing Systems 30*, pages 5998–6008. Curran Associates, Inc.

Ravi Kumar Venkatesh. 2013. Legal documents clustering and summarization using hierarchical latent dirichlet allocation. *IAES International Journal of Artificial Intelligence*, 2(1).

Yonghui Wu, Mike Schuster, Zhifeng Chen, Quoc V. Le, Mohammad Norouzi, Wolfgang Macherey, Maxim Krikun, Yuan Cao, Qin Gao, Klaus Macherey, Jeff Klingner, Apurva Shah, Melvin Johnson, Xiaobing Liu, ukasz Kaiser, Stephan Gouws, Yoshikiyo Kato, Taku Kudo, Hideto Kazawa, Keith Stevens, George Kurian, Nishant Patil, Wei Wang, Cliff Young, Jason Smith, Jason Riesa, Alex Rudnick, Oriol Vinyals, Greg Corrado, Macduff Hughes, and Jeffrey Dean. 2016. Google's neural machine translation system: Bridging the gap between human and machine translation. *CoRR*, abs/1609.08144.

Daniel Taylor Young. 2013. How do you measure a constitutional moment? using algorithmic topic modeling to evaluate bruce ackerman's theory of constitutional change. *Yale Law Journal*, 122:1990.

A Appendices

A.1 Data Parsing

The original scraped dataset had 6,839 judgments in PDF format. The PDFs were parsed with a custom Python script using the `pdfplumber`[5] library. For the purposes of our experiments, we excluded the case information section found at the beginning of each PDF as we did not consider it to be part of the judgment (this section contains information such as Case Number, Decision Date, Coram, Counsel Names etc). The labels were extracted based on their location in the first page of

---

[5]`https://github.com/jsvine/pdfplumber`

the PDF, i.e. immediately after the case information section and before the author line. After this process, 611 judgments that were originally unlabelled and one incorrectly parsed judgment were dropped, leaving the final dataset of 6,227 judgments.

A.2 Label Mappings

Labels are a double-dash-delimited series of increasingly specific legal N-grams (e.g. "tort–negligence–duty of care–whether occupier owes lawful entrants a duty of care"), which denote increasingly specific and narrow areas of law. Multiple labels are expressed in multiple lines (one label per line). We checked the topic labels for consistency and typographical errors by inspecting a list of unique labels across the dataset. Erroneous labels and labels that were conceptual subsets of others were manually mapped to primary labels via the mapping presented in Table 5. Some subjectivity admittedly exists in the choice of mappings. However we were not aware of any standard ontology for used for legal area classification, particularly for Singapore law. To mitigate this, we based the primary label set on the Singapore Academy of Law Subject Tree which, for copyright reasons, we were unable to reproduce here.

It was only *after* this step that the top 30 labels were kept and the remaining mapped to "others". Figure 1 presents all 51 original labels and their frequencies.

A.3 Implementation Details on Models Used

All text preprocessing (tokenization, stopping, and lemmatization) was done using `spaCy` defaults (Honnibal and Montani, 2017).

A.3.1 Baseline Models

$count_m$ uses the FlashText algorithm for efficient exact phrase matching within long judgment texts (Singh, 2017). To populate the set of associated terms for each label, all sub-labels attributable to the label within the given training subset were first added as exact phrases. Next, the label itself was tokenized into unigrams. Each unigram was added individually to the set of associated terms unless it fell within a set of customized stopwords we created after inspecting all labels. The set is $\{and, law, of, non, others\}$.

Beyond $count_{25}$, we experimented with thresholds of 1, 5, 10, and 35 occurrences. F1 scores increased linearly as thresholds increased from 1

Primary Label	Alternative Labels
administrative_and_constitutional_law	administrative_law, adminstrative_law, constitutional_interpretation, constitutional_law, elections
admiralty_shipping_and_aviation_law	admiralty, admiralty_and_shipping, carriage_of_goods_by_air_and_land
agency_law	agency
arbitration	
banking_law	banking
biomedic_law_and_ethics	
building_and_construction_law	building_and_construction_contracts
civil_procedure	civil_procedue, application_for_summary_judgment, limitation_of_actions, procedure, discovery_of_documents
company_law	companies, companies-_meetings, companies_-_winding_up
competition_law	
conflict_of_laws	conflicts_of_laws, conflicts_of_law
contract_law	commercial_transactions, contract, contract_-_interpretation, contracts, transactions
criminal_law	contempt_of_court, offences, rape
criminal_procedure_and_sentencing	criminal_procedure, criminal_sentencing, sentencing, bail
credit_and_security	credit_and_securities, credit_&_security
damages	damage, damages_-_assessment, injunction, injunctions
evidence	evidence_law
employment_law	work_injury_compensation_act
equity_and_trusts	equity, estoppel, trusts, tracing
family_law	succession_and_wills, probate_&_administration, probate_and_administration
insolvency_law	insolvency
insurance_law	insurance
intellectual_property_law	intellectual_property, copyright, copyright_infringement, designs, trade_marks_and_trade_names, trade_marks, trademarks, patents_and_inventions
international_law	
non_land_property_law	personal_property, property_law, choses_in_action
land_law	landlord_and_tenant, land, planning_law
legal_profession	legal_professional
muslim_law	
partnership_law	partnership, partnerships
restitution	
revenue_and_tax_law	tax, revenue_law, tax_law
tort_law	tort, abuse_of_process
words_and_phrases	statutory_interpretation
res_judicata	
immigration	
courts_and_jurisdiction	
road_traffic	
debt_and_recovery	
bailment	
charities	
unincorporated_associations_and_trade_unions	unincorporated_associations
professions	
bills_of_exchange_and_other_negotiable_instruments	
gifts	
mental_disorders_and_treatment	
deeds_and_other_instruments	
financial_and_securities_markets	
sheriffs_and_bailiffs	
betting	_gaming_and_lotteries, gaming_and_lotteries
sale_of_goods	
time	

Table 5: Primary-Alternative mappings for raw dataset labels

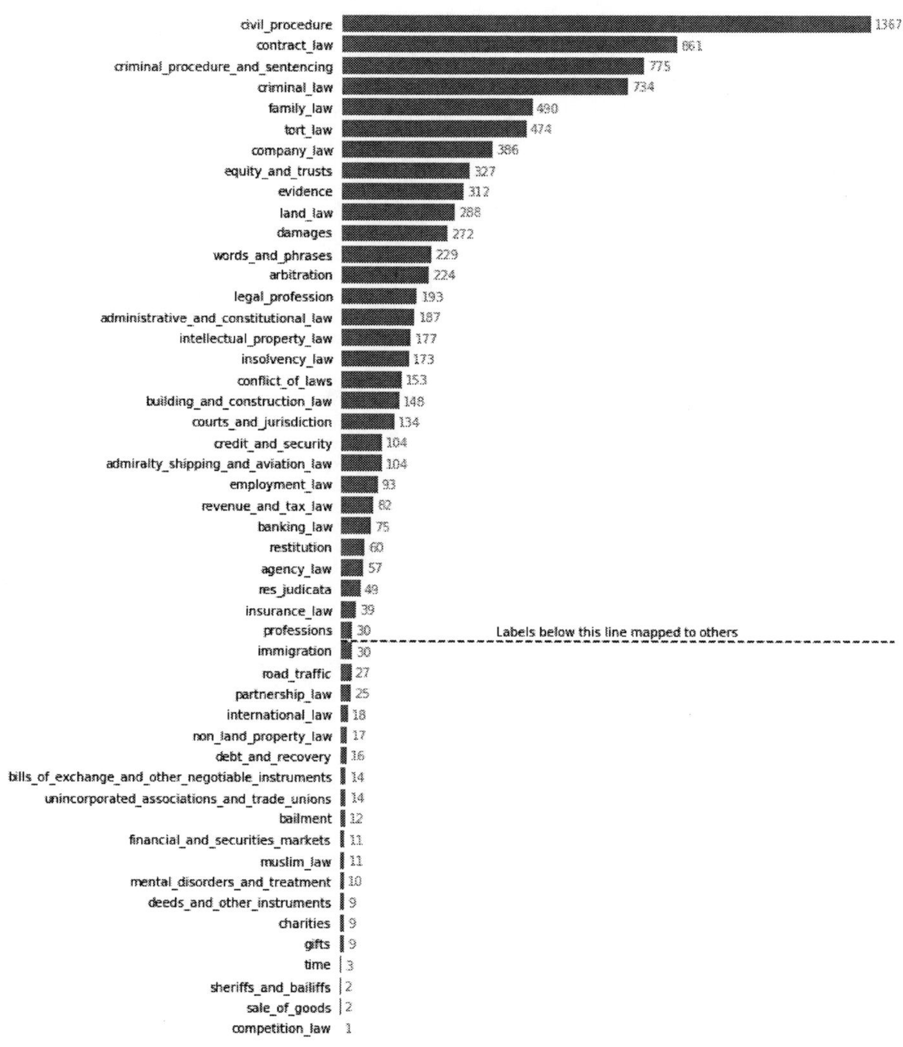

Figure 1: Distribution of Cleaned Labels and the Final 30 Labels Included

to 25, but only increased marginally from 25 to 35.

A.3.2 Topic Models

LSA was achieved using scikit-learn's TFIDFVectorizer and TruncatedSVD classes. Document-topic weights were then normalized with scikit-learn's Normalizer class before being fed to the classifier. Where relevant, the random state was set at 36. Note that judgments were preprocessed with spaCy as above before being fed into the LSA pipeline. Beyond 100 and 250 topics, an experiment using 50 topics only performed consistently worse.

The classifier used scikit-learn's OneVsRest and LinearSVC classes with all default settings. An alternative linSVM with balanced class-weights was tested but performed consistently worse by both macro and micro-f1 scores and was thus omitted for brevity.

A.3.3 Word Embedding Feature Models

For all the word embedding feature models, we used spaCy's tokenizer to obtain the word tokens. We fixed the maximum sequence length per judgment at 10K tokens and used a vocabulary of the top 60K most common words in the training corpus. Words that did not have a corresponding GloVe vector were initialized from a uniform distribution with range $[-0.5, 0.5]$. The models were implemented in TensorFlow[6] with the Keras API. To deal with class imbalance, we weighted the losses by passing class weights to the `class_weight` argument of `model.fit`.

For the CNN models, we based our implementation off the non-static version in Kim (2014) but used [3, 3, 3] x 600 filters, as we found that increasing the number of filters improved results.

A.3.4 BERT

To fine-tune BERT to our multi-label classification task, we used the PyTorch implementation of BERT by `HuggingFace`[7] and added a linear classification layer $W \in \mathbf{R}^{K \times H}$, where K is the number of classifier labels and H is the dimension of the pooled representation of the input sequence, followed by a sigmoid function. We fine-tuned all the BERT models using mixed-precision training and gradient accumulation (8

steps). To address data imbalance, we weighted the losses by passing positive weights for each class (capped at 30) to the `pos_weight` argument of `torch.nn.BCEWithLogitsLoss`.

A.3.5 ULMFiT

We first fine-tuned the pre-trained ULMFiT language model (WikiText-103) on our entire corpus of 6,227 judgments using a language model objective for 10 epochs before replacing the output layer with a classifier output layer and then further fine-tuned the model on labelled data with the classification objective using `fastai`'s recommended recipe[8] for text classification (we used gradual unfreezing and the one-cycle learning rate schedule to fine-tune the classifier until there was no more improvement on the validation score). We used mixed precision training and fixed the maximum sequence length at 5K tokens to allow the training data to fit in memory.

A.4 Topics Extracted by Topic Mining

Table 6 presents the top 10 tokens associated with the top 25 topics extracted by LSA on the 100% data subset. Notice that these topics are common to both lsa_{100} and lsa_{250} since the output of TFIDF and SVD do not vary with k. The only difference is that lsa_{100} uses only the first 100 topic vectors (i.e. the topic vectors corresponding to the 100 largest singular values computed by the decomposition) created by LSA whereas lsa_{250} uses the first 250. However, topics extracted from different data subsets would differ.

A quick perusal of the extract topics suggests many have would be highly informative of a case's legal area. Topics 2, 7, 21, 24, and 25 map nicely to criminal law, topics 3 and 5 to family law, and topics 18, and 20 to arbitration. Other individually-informative topics include topics 6 (road traffic), 8 (building and construction law), 9 (land law), 11 (legal profession), 16 (company law), and 22 (conflict of laws).

---

[6] `https://github.com/tensorflow/tensorflow`

[7] `https://github.com/huggingface/pytorch-pretrained-BERT`

[8] `https://docs.fast.ai/text.html`

Topic No.	Top 10 Tokens
1	plaintiff, court, defendant, case, party, claim, order, appeal, fact, time
2	offence, accuse, sentence, imprisonment, prosecution, offender, charge, drug, convict, conviction
3	matrimonial, husband, wife, marriage, child, maintenance, contribution, asset, cpf, divorce
4	application, court, appeal, order, district, matrimonial, respondent, proceeding, judge, file
5	matrimonial, marriage, child, maintenance, husband, divorce, parliament, division, context, broad
6	injury, accident, plaintiff, damage, defendant, dr, award, medical, work, pain
7	drug, cnb, diamorphine, packet, mda, bag, heroin, traffic, arbitration, plastic
8	contractor, contract, sentence, imprisonment, construction, clause, project, offender, cl, payment
9	property, land, purchaser, tenant, title, estate, decease, owner, road, lease
10	arbitration, victim, rape, sexual, arbitrator, arbitral, cane, clause, accuse, cl
11	disciplinary, profession, solicitor, committee, advocate, society, client, misconduct, lpa, professional
12	creditor, debt, bankruptcy, accident, debtor, wind, liquidator, injury, death, decease
13	plaintiff, defendant, proprietor, infringement, plaintiffs, defendants, cane, 2014, land, 2012
14	appellant, 2014, road, district, 2016, trial, defendant, property, judge, pp
15	drug, arbitration, profession, disciplinary, society, clause, vessel, death, advocate, diamorphine
16	shareholder, director, company, vehicle, share, resolution, traffic, management, vote, minority
17	creditor, solicitor, road, vehicle, profession, bankruptcy, disciplinary, drive, lane, driver
18	arbitration, adjudicator, decease, tribunal, adjudication, arbitral, vehicle, arbitrator, drive, mark
19	contractor, adjudicator, adjudication, decease, beneficiary, estate, employer, death, child, executor
20	arbitration, arbitrator, tribunal, award, arbitral, profession, contractor, disciplinary, architect, lpa
21	drug, respondent, appellant, diamorphine, gd, factor, cl, adjudicator, judge, creditor
22	2015, forum, 2014, 2016, 2013, foreign, 2012, appellant, conveniens, spiliada
23	stay, appellant, arbitration, estate, register, forum, district, beneficiary, owner, applicant
24	vessel, cargo, decease, murder, sale, ship, death, dr, kill, knife
25	sexual, rape, penis, vagina, complainant, stroke, intercourse, penetration, vessel, sex

Table 6: Top Tokens For Top 25 Topics Extracted by lsa_{250} on the 100% subset.

Extreme Multi-Label Legal Text Classification:
A case study in EU Legislation

Ilias Chalkidis*   Manos Fergadiotis*   Prodromos Malakasiotis*
Nikolaos Aletras   Ion Androutsopoulos***
* Department of Informatics, Athens University of Economics and Business, Greece
** Computer Science Department, University of Sheffield, UK
[ihalk,fergadiotis,rulller,ion]@aueb.gr, n.aletras@sheffield.ac.uk

Abstract

We consider the task of Extreme Multi-Label Text Classification (XMTC) in the legal domain. We release a new dataset of 57k legislative documents from EUR-LEX, the European Union's public document database, annotated with concepts from EUROVOC, a multi-disciplinary thesaurus. The dataset is substantially larger than previous EUR-LEX datasets and suitable for XMTC, few-shot and zero-shot learning. Experimenting with several neural classifiers, we show that BIGRUs with self-attention outperform the current multi-label state-of-the-art methods, which employ label-wise attention. Replacing CNNs with BIGRUs in label-wise attention networks leads to the best overall performance.

1 Introduction

Extreme multi-label text classification (XMTC), is the task of tagging documents with relevant labels from an extremely large label set, typically containing thousands of labels (classes). Applications include building web directories (Partalas et al., 2015), labeling scientific publications with concepts from ontologies (Tsatsaronis et al., 2015), product categorization (McAuley and Leskovec, 2013), categorizing medical examinations (Mullenbach et al., 2018; Rios and Kavuluru, 2018b), and indexing legal documents (Mencia and Frnkranz, 2007). We focus on legal text processing, an emerging NLP field with many applications (Nallapati and Manning, 2008; Aletras et al., 2016; Chalkidis et al., 2017), but limited publicly available resources.

We release a new dataset, named EURLEX57K, including 57,000 English documents of EU legislation from the EUR-LEX portal. All documents have been tagged with concepts from the European Vocabulary (EUROVOC), maintained by the Publications Office of the European Union. Although EUROVOC contains more than 7,000 concepts, most of them are rarely used in practice. Consequently, they are under-represented in EURLEX57K, making the dataset also appropriate for few-shot and zero-shot learning.

Experimenting on EURLEX57K, we explore the use of various RNN-based and CNN-based neural classifiers, including the state of the art Label-Wise Attention Network of Mullenbach et al. (2018), called CNN-LWAN here. We show that both a simpler BIGRU with self-attention (Xu et al., 2015) and the Hierarchical Attention Network (HAN) of Yang et al. (2016) outperform CNN-LWAN by a wide margin. Replacing the CNN encoder of CNN-LWAN with a BIGRU, which leads to a method we call BIGRU-LWAN, further improves performance. Similar findings are observed in the zero-shot setting where Z-BIGRU-LWAN outperforms Z-CNN-LWAN.

2 Related Work

Liu et al. (2017) proposed a CNN similar to that of Kim (2014) for XMTC. They reported results on several benchmark datasets, most notably: RCV1 (Lewis et al., 2004), containing news articles; EUR-LEX (Mencia and Frnkranz, 2007), containing legal documents; Amazon-12K (McAuley and Leskovec, 2013), containing product descriptions; and Wiki-30K (Zubiaga, 2012), containing Wikipedia articles. Their proposed method outperformed both tree-based methods (e.g., FASTXML, (Prabhu and Varma, 2014)) and target-embedding methods (e.g., SLEEC (Bhatia et al., 2015), FASTTEXT (Bojanowski et al., 2016)).

RNNs with self-attention have been employed in a wide variety of NLP tasks, such as Natural Language Inference (Liu et al., 2016), Textual Entail-

Proceedings of the Natural Legal Language Processing Workshop 2019, pages 78–87
Minneapolis, Minesotta, June 7, 2019. ©2019 Association for Computational Linguistics

ment (Rocktäschel et al., 2016), and Text Classification (Zhou et al., 2016). You et al. (2018) used RNNs with self-attention in XMTC comparing with tree-based methods and deep learning approaches including vanilla LSTMs and CNNs. Their method outperformed the other approaches in three out of four XMTC datasets, demonstrating the effectiveness of attention-based RNNs.

Mullenbach et al. (2018) investigated the use of label-wise attention mechanisms in medical code prediction on the MIMIC-II and MIMIC-III datasets (Johnson et al., 2017). MIMIC-II and MIMIC-III contain over 20,000 and 47,000 documents tagged with approximately 9,000 and 5,000 ICD-9 code descriptors, respectively. Their best method, Convolutional Attention for Multi-Label Classification, called CNN-LWAN here, includes multiple attention mechanisms, one for each one of the L labels. CNN-LWAN outperformed weak baselines, namely logistic regression, vanilla BIGRUs and CNNs. Another important fact is that CNN-LWAN was found to have the best interpretability in comparison with the rest of the methods in human readers' evaluation.

Rios and Kavuluru (2018b) discuss the challenge of few-shot and zero-shot learning on the MIMIC datasets. Over 50% of all ICD-9 labels never appear in MIMIC-III, while 5,000 labels occur fewer than 10 times. The same authors proposed a new method, named Zero-Shot Attentive CNN, called Z-CNN-LWAN here, which is similar to CNN-LWAN (Mullenbach et al., 2018), but also exploits the provided ICD-9 code descriptors. The proposed Z-CNN-LWAN method was compared with prior state-of-the-art methods, including CNN-LWAN (Mullenbach et al., 2018) and MATCH-CNN (Rios and Kavuluru, 2018a), a multi-head matching CNN. While Z-CNN-LWAN did not outperform CNN-LWAN overall on MIMIC-II and MIMIC-III, it had exceptional results in few-shot and zero-shot learning, being able to identify labels with few or no instances at all in the training sets. Experimental results showed an improvement of approximately four orders of magnitude in comparison with CNN-LWAN in few-shot learning and an impressive 0.269 $R@5$ in zero-shot learning, compared to zero $R@5$ reported for the other models compared.[1] Rios and Kavuluru (2018b) also apply graph convolutions to hierarchical relations of the labels, which improves the perfor-

mance on few-shot and zero-shot learning. In this work, we do not consider relations between labels and do not discuss this method further.

Note that CNN-LWAN and Z-CNN-LWAN were not compared so far with strong generic text classification baselines. Both Mullenbach et al. (2018) and Rios and Kavuluru (2018b) proposed sophisticated attention-based architectures, which intuitively are a good fit for XMTC, but they did not directly compare those models with RNNs with self-attention (You et al., 2018) or even more complex architectures, such as Hierarchical Attention Networks (HANs) (Yang et al., 2016).

3 EUROVOC & EURLEX57K

3.1 EUROVOC Thesaurus

EUROVOC is a multilingual thesaurus maintained by the Publications Office of the European Union.[2] It is used by the European Parliament, the national and regional parliaments in Europe, some national government departments, and other European organisations. The current version of EUROVOC contains more than 7,000 concepts referring to various activities of the EU and its Member States (e.g., economics, health-care, trade, etc.). It has also been used for indexing documents in systems of EU institutions, e.g., in web legislative databases, such as EUR-LEX and CELLAR. All EUROVOC concepts are represented as tuples called *descriptors*, each containing a unique numeric identifier and a (possibly) multi-word description of the concept concept, for example (1309, import), (693, citrus fruit), (192, health control), (863, Spain), (2511, agri-monetary policy).

3.2 EURLEX57K

EURLEX57K can be viewed as an improved version of the EUR-LEX dataset released by Mencia and Frnkranz (2007), which included 19,601 documents tagged with 3,993 different EUROVOC concepts. While EUR-LEX has been widely used in XMTC research, it is less than half the size of EURLEX57K and one of the smallest among XMTC benchmarks.[3] Over the past years the EUR-LEX archive has been widely expanded. EURLEX57K is a more up to date dataset including 57,000 pieces

---

[1]See Section 5.2 for a definition of $R@K$.

[2]https://publications.europa.eu/en/web/eu-vocabularies

[3]The most notable XMTC benchmarks can be found at http://manikvarma.org/downloads/XC/XMLRepository.html.

of EU legislation from the EUR-LEX portal.[4] All documents have been annotated by the Publications Office of EU with multiple concepts from the EUROVOC thesaurus. EURLEX57K is split in training (45,000 documents), development (6,000), and validation (6,000) subsets (see Table 1).[5]

Subset	Documents (D)	Words/D	Labels/D
Train	45,000	729	5
Dev.	6,000	714	5
Test	6,000	725	5

Table 1: Statistics of the EUR-LEX dataset.

All documents are structured in four major zones: the *header* including the title and the name of the legal body that enforced the legal act; the *recitals* that consist of references in the legal background of the decision; the *main body*, which is usually organized in articles; and the *attachments* that usually include appendices and annexes. For simplicity, we will refer to each one of *header*, *recitals*, *attachments* and each of the *main body*'s articles as *sections*. We have pre-processed all documents in order to provide the aforementioned structure.

While EUROVOC includes over 7,000 concepts (labels), only 4,271 (59.31%) of them are present in EURLEX57K. Another important fact is that most labels are under-represented; only 2,049 (47,97%) have been assigned to more than 10 documents. Such an aggressive Zipfian distribution (Figure 1) has also been noted in other domains, like medical examinations (Rios and Kavuluru, 2018b) where XMTC has been applied to index documents with concepts from medical thesauri.

The labels of EURLEX57K are divided in three categories: *frequent* labels (746), which occur in more than 50 training documents and can be found in all three subsets (training, development, test); *few-shot* labels (3,362), which appear in 1 to 50 training documents; and *zero-shot* labels (163), which appear in the development and/or test, but not in the training, documents.

4 Methods Considered

We experiment with a wide repertoire of methods including linear and non-linear neural classifiers. We also propose and conduct initial experiments

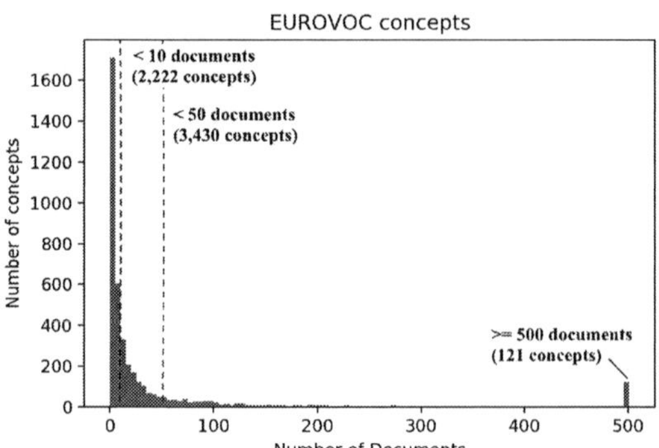

Figure 1: EUROVOC concepts frequency.

with two novel neural methods that aim to cope with the extended length of the legal documents and the information sparsity (for XMTC purposes) across the *sections* of the documents.

4.1 Baselines

4.1.1 Exact Match

To demonstrate that plain label name matching is not sufficient, our first weak baseline, Exact Match, tags documents only with labels whose descriptors appear verbatim in the documents.

4.1.2 Logistic Regression

To demonstrate the limitations of linear classifiers with bag-of-words representations, we train a Logistic Regression classifier with TF-IDF scores for the most frequent unigrams, bigrams, trigrams, 4-grams, 5-grams across all documents. Logistic regression with similar features has been widely used for multi-label classification in the past.

4.2 Neural Approaches

We present eight alternative neural methods. In the following subsections, we describe their structure consisting of five main parts:

- *word encoder* (ENC_w): turns word embeddings into context-aware embeddings,

- *section encoder* (ENC_s): turns each section (sentence) into a sentence embedding,

- *document encoder* (ENC_d): turns an entire document into a final dense representation,

- *section decoder* (DEC_s) or *document decoder* (DEC_d): maps the section or document representation to a many-hot label assignment.

All parts except for ENC_w and DEC_d are optional, i.e., they may not be present in all methods.

---

[4] https://eur-lex.europa.eu

[5] Our dataset is available at http://nlp.cs. aueb.gr/software_and_datasets/EURLEX57K, with permission of reuse under European Union©, https://eur-lex.europa.eu, 1998–2019.

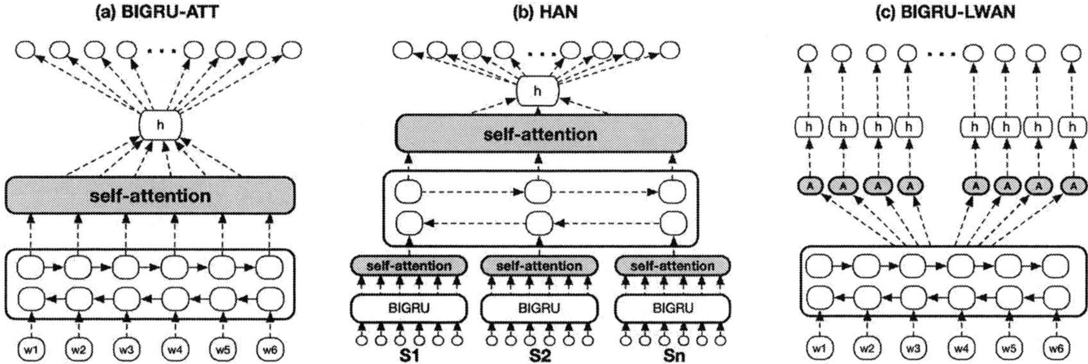

Figure 2: Illustration of (a) BIGRU-ATT, (b) HAN, and (c) BIGRU-LWAN.

4.2.1 BIGRU-ATT

In the first deep learning method, BIGRU-ATT (Figure 2a), ENC_w is a stack of BIGRUs that converts the pre-trained word embeddings (w_t) to context-aware ones (h_t). ENC_d employs a self attention mechanism to produce the final representation d of the document as a weighted sum of h_t:

$$a_t = \frac{\exp(h_t^\top u)}{\sum_j \exp(h_j^\top u)} \qquad (1)$$

$$d = \frac{1}{T} \sum_{t=1}^{T} a_t h_t \qquad (2)$$

T is the document's length in words, and u is a trainable vector used to compute the attention scores a_t over h_t. DEC_d is a linear layer with $L = 4,271$ output units and sigmoid (σ) activations that maps the document representation d to L probabilities, one per label.

4.2.2 HAN

The Hierarchical Attention Network (HAN) (Yang et al., 2016), exploits the structure of the documents by encoding the text in two consecutive steps (Figure 2b). First, a BIGRU (ENC_w) followed by a self-attention mechanism (ENC_s) turns the word embeddings (w_{it}) of each section s_i with T_i words into a section embedding c_i:

$$v_{it} = \tanh(W^{(s)} h_{it} + b^{(s)}) \qquad (3)$$

$$a_{it}^{(s)} = \frac{\exp(v_{it}^\top u^{(s)})}{\sum_j \exp(v_{ij}^\top u^{(s)})} \qquad (4)$$

$$c_i = \frac{1}{T_i} \sum_{t=1}^{T_i} a_{it}^{(s)} h_{it} \qquad (5)$$

where $u^{(s)}$ is a trainable vector. Next, ENC_d, another BIGRU with self-attention, converts the section embeddings (S in total, as many as the sections) to the final document representation d:

$$v_i = \tanh(W^{(d)} c_i + b^{(d)}) \qquad (6)$$

$$a_i^{(d)} = \frac{\exp(v_i^\top u^{(d)})}{\sum_j \exp(v_j^\top u^{(d)})} \qquad (7)$$

$$d = \frac{1}{S} \sum_{i=1}^{S} a_i^{(d)} c_i \qquad (8)$$

where $u^{(d)}$ is a trainable vector. The final decoder DEC_d of HAN is the same as in BIGRU-ATT.

4.3 MAX-HSS

Initial experiments we conducted indicated that HAN is outperformed by the shallower BIGRU-ATT. We suspected that the main reason was the fact that the section embeddings c_i that HAN's ENC_s produces contain useful information that is later degraded by HAN's ENC_d. Based on this assumption, we experimented with a novel method, named Max-Pooling over Hierarchical Attention Scorers (MAX-HSS). MAX-HSS produces section embeddings c_i in the same way as HAN, but then employs a separate DEC_s per section to produce label predictions from each section embedding c_i:

$$p_i^{(s)} = \sigma(W^{(m)} c_i + b^{(m)}) \qquad (9)$$

where p_i is an L-dimensional vector containing probabilities for all labels, derived from c_i. DEC_d aggregates the predictions for the whole document with a MAXPOOL operator that extracts the highest probability per label across all sections:

$$p^{(d)} = \text{MAXPOOL}(p_1^{(s)}, \ldots, p_S^{(s)}) \qquad (10)$$

Intuitively, each section tries to predict the labels relying on its content independently, and DEC_d extracts the most probable labels across sections.

4.3.1 CNN-LWAN and BIGRU-LWAN

The Label-wise Attention Network, LWAN (Mullenbach et al., 2018), also uses a self-attention mechanism, but here ENC_d employs L independent attention heads, one per label, generating L document representations $d_l = \sum_t a_{lt} h_t$ ($l = 1, \ldots, L$) from the sequence of context aware word embeddings $h_1, \ldots, h_T$ of each document d. The intuition is that each attention head focuses on possibly different aspects of $h_1, \ldots, h_T$ needed to decide if the corresponding label should be assigned to the document or not. DEC_d employs L linear layers with σ activation, each one operating on a label-wise document representation d_l to produce the probability for the corresponding label. In the original LWAN (Mullenbach et al., 2018), called CNN-LWAN here, ENC_w is a vanilla CNN. We use a modified version, BIGRU-LWAN, where ENC_w is a BIGRU (Figure 2c).

4.4 Z-CNN-LWAN and Z-BIGRU-LWAN

Following the work of Mullenbach et al. (2018), Rios and Kavuluru (2018b) designed a similar architecture in order to improve the results in documents that are classified with rare labels. In one of their models, ENC_d creates label representations, u_l, from the corresponding descriptors as follows:

$$u_l = \frac{1}{E} \sum_{e=1}^{E} w_{le} \tag{11}$$

where w_{le} is the word embedding of the e-th word in the l-th label descriptor. The label representations are then used as alternative attention vectors:

$$v_t = \tanh(W^{(z)} h_t + b^{(z)}) \tag{12}$$

$$a_{lt} = \frac{\exp(v_t^\top u_l)}{\sum_j \exp(v_j^\top u_l)} \tag{13}$$

$$d_l = \frac{1}{T} \sum_{t=1}^{T} a_{lt} h_t \tag{14}$$

where h_t are the context-aware embeddings produced by a vanilla CNN (ENC_w) operating on the document's word embeddings, a_{lt} are the attention scores conditioned on the corresponding label representation u_l, and d_l is the label-wise document representation. DEC_d also relies on label representations to produce each label's probability:

$$p_l = \sigma(u_l^\top d_l) \tag{15}$$

Note that the representations u_l of both encountered (during training) and unseen (zero-shot) labels remain unchanged, because the word embeddings w_{le} are not updated (Eq. 11). This keeps the representations of zero-shot labels close to those of encountered labels they share several descriptor words with. In turn, this helps the attention mechanism (Eq. 13) and the decoder (Eq. 15), where the label representations u_l are used, cope with unseen labels that have similar descriptors with encountered labels. As with CNN-LWAN and BIGRU-LWAN, we experiment with the original version of the model of Rios and Kavuluru (2018b), which uses a CNN ENC_w (Z-CNN-LWAN), and a version that uses a BIGRU ENC_w (Z-BIGRU-LWAN).

4.5 LW-HAN

We also propose a new method, Label-Wise Hierarchical Attention Network (LW-HAN), that combines ideas from both HAN and LWAN. For each section, LW-HAN employs an LWAN to produce L probabilities. Then, like MAX-HSS, a MAXPOOL operator extracts the highest probability per label across all sections. In effect, LW-HAN exploits the document structure to cope with the extended document length of legal documents, while employing multiple label-wise attention heads to deal with the vast and sparse label set. By contrast, MAX-HSS does not use label-wise attention.

5 Experimental Results

5.1 Experimental Setup

We implemented all methods in KERAS.[6] We used Adam (Kingma and Ba, 2015) with learning rate $1e - 3$. Hyper-parameters were tuned on development data using HYPEROPT.[7] We tuned for the following hyper-parameters and ranges: ENC output units $\{200, 300, 400\}$, ENC layers $\{1, 2\}$, batch size $\{8, 12, 16\}$, dropout rate $\{0.1, 0.2, 0.3, 0.4\}$, word dropout rate $\{0.0, 0.01, 0.02\}$. For the best hyper-parameter values, we perform five runs and report mean scores on test data. For statistical significance, we take the run of each method with the best performance on development data, and perform two-tailed approximate randomization tests

---

[6] https://keras.io/
[7] https://github.com/hyperopt

(Dror et al., 2018) on test data. We used 200-dimensional pre-trained GLOVE embeddings (Pennington et al., 2014) in all neural methods.

5.2 Evaluation Measures

The most common evaluation measures in XMTC are recall ($R@K$), precision ($P@K$), and *nDCG* (*nDCG@K*) at the top K predicted labels, along with micro-averaged F-1 across all labels. Measures that macro-average over labels do not consider the number of instances per label, thus being very sensitive to infrequent labels, which are many more than frequent ones (Section 3.2). On the other hand, ranking measures, like $R@K$, $P@K$, *nDCG@K*, are sensitive to the choice of K. In EURLEX57K the average number of labels per document is 5.07, hence evaluating at $K = 5$ is a reasonable choice. We note that 99.4% of the dataset's documents have at most 10 gold labels.

While $R@K$ and $P@K$ are commonly used, we question their suitability for XMTC. $R@K$ leads to unfair penalization of methods when documents have more than K gold labels. Evaluating at $K = 1$ for a document with $N > 1$ gold labels returns at most $R@1 = \frac{1}{N}$, unfairly penalizing systems by not allowing them to return N labels. This is shown in Figure 3, where the green lines show that $R@K$ decreases as K decreases, because of low scores obtained for documents with more than K labels. On the other hand, $P@K$ leads to excessive penalization for documents with fewer than K gold labels. Evaluating at $K = 5$ for a document with just one gold label returns at most $P@5 = \frac{1}{5} = 0.20$, unfairly penalizing systems that retrieved all the gold labels (in this case, just one). The red lines of Figure 3 decline as K increases, because the number of documents with fewer than K gold labels increases (recall that the average number of gold labels is 5.07).

Similar concerns have led to the introduction of R-Precision and *nDCG@K* in Information Retrieval (Manning et al., 2009), which we believe are also more appropriate for XMTC. Note, however, that R-Precision requires that the number of gold labels per document is known beforehand, which is not realistic in practical applications. Therefore we propose R-Precision@K ($RP@K$) where K is the maximum number of retrieved labels. Both $RP@K$ and *nDCG@K* adjust to the number of gold labels per document, without unfairly penalizing systems for documents with

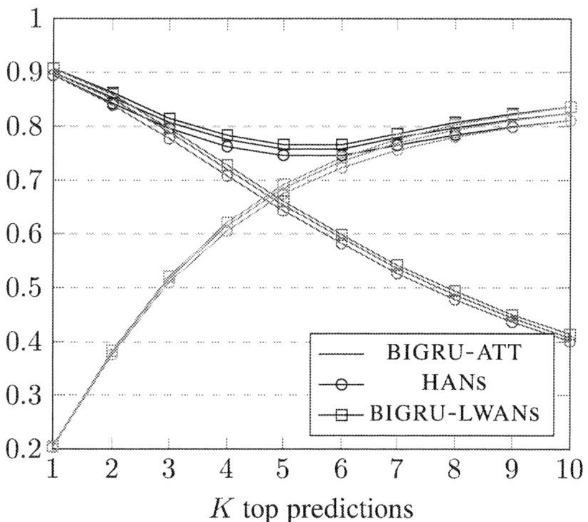

Figure 3: $R@K$ (green lines), $P@K$ (red), $RP@K$ (black) scores of the best methods (BIGRU-ATT, HANs, BIGRU-LWAN), for $K = 1$ to 10. All scores macro-averaged over test documents.

fewer than K or many more than K gold labels. They are defined as follows:

$$RP@K = \frac{1}{N} \sum_{n=1}^{N} \sum_{k=1}^{K} \frac{\mathrm{Rel}(n, k)}{\min(K, R_n)} \quad (16)$$

$$nDCG@K = \frac{1}{N} \sum_{n=1}^{N} Z_{Kn} \sum_{k=1}^{K} \frac{2^{\mathrm{Rel}(n,k)} - 1}{\log_2(1 + k)} \quad (17)$$

Here N is the number of test documents; $\mathrm{Rel}(n, k)$ is 1 if the k-th retrieved label of the n-th test document is correct, otherwise 0; R_n is the number of gold labels of the n-th test document; and Z_{Kn} is a normalization factor to ensure that *nDCG@K* = 1 for perfect ranking.

In effect, $RP@K$ is a macro-averaged (over test documents) version of $P@K$, but K is reduced to the number of gold labels R_n of each test document, if K exceeds R_n. Figure 3 shows $RP@K$ for the three best systems. Unlike $P@K$, $RP@K$ does not decline sharply as K increases, because it replaces K by R_n (number of gold labels) when $K > R_n$. For $K = 1$, $RP@K$ is equivalent to $P@K$, as confirmed by Fig. 3. For large values of K that almost always exceed R_n, $RP@K$ asymptotically approaches $R@K$ (macro-averaged over documents), as also confirmed by Fig. 3.

5.3 Overall Experimental Results

Table 2 reports experimental results for all methods and evaluation measures. As expected, Exact Match is vastly outperformed by machine learning

	ALL LABELS			FREQUENT		FEW		ZERO	
	$RP@5$	$nDCG@5$	Micro-$F1$	$RP@5$	$nDCG@5$	$RP@5$	$nDCG@5$	$RP@5$	$nDCG@5$
Exact Match	0.097	0.099	0.120	0.219	0.201	0.111	0.074	0.194	0.186
Logistic Regression	0.710	0.741	0.539	0.767	0.781	0.508	0.470	0.011	0.011
BIGRU-ATT	0.758	0.789	0.689	0.799	0.813	0.631	0.580	0.040	0.027
HAN	0.746	0.778	0.680	0.789	0.805	0.597	0.544	0.051	0.034
CNN-LWAN	0.716	0.746	0.642	0.761	0.772	0.613	0.557	0.036	0.023
BIGRU-LWAN	**0.766**	**0.796**	**0.698**	**0.805**	**0.819**	**0.662**	**0.618**	0.029	0.019
Z-CNN-LWAN	0.684	0.717	0.618	0.730	0.745	0.495	0.454	0.321	0.264
Z-BIGRU-LWAN	0.718	0.752	0.652	0.764	0.780	0.561	0.510	**0.438**	**0.345**
ENSEMBLE-LWAN	**0.766**	**0.796**	**0.698**	**0.805**	**0.819**	**0.662**	**0.618**	**0.438**	**0.345**
MAX-HSS	0.737	0.773	0.671	0.784	0.803	0.463	0.443	0.039	0.028
LW-HAN	0.721	0.761	0.669	0.766	0.790	0.412	0.402	0.039	0.026

Table 2: Results on EURLEX57K for all, frequent (> 50 training instances), few-shot (1 to 50 instances), and zero-shot labels. All the differences between the best (bold) and other methods are statistically significant ($p < 0.01$).

methods, while Logistic Regression is also unable to cope with the complexity of XMTC.

In Section 2, we referred to the lack of previous experimental comparison between methods relying on label-wise attention and strong generic text classification baselines. Interestingly, for all, frequent, and even few-shot labels, the generic BIGRU-ATT performs better than CNN-LWAN, which was designed for XMTC. HAN also performs better than CNN-LWAN for all and frequent labels. However, replacing the CNN encoder of CNN-LWAN with a BIGRU (BIGRU-LWAN) leads to the best results overall, with the exception of zero-shot labels, indicating that the main weakness of CNN-LWAN is its vanilla CNN encoder.

5.4 Few-shot and Zero-shot Results

As noted by Rios and Kavuluru (2018b), developing reliable and robust classifiers for few-shot and zero-shot tasks is a significant challenge. Consider, for example, a test document referring to concepts that have rarely (few-shot) or never (zero-shot) occurred in training documents (e.g., 'tropical disease', which exists once in the whole dataset). A reliable classifier should be able to at least make a good guess for such rare concepts.

As shown in Table 2, BIGRU-LWAN outperforms all other methods in both frequent and few-shotlabels, but not in zero-shot labels, where Z-CNN-LWAN (Rios and Kavuluru, 2018b) provides exceptional results compared to other methods. Again, replacing the vanilla CNN of Z-CNN-LWAN with a BIGRU (Z-BIGRU-LWAN) improves performance across all label types and measures.

All other methods, including BIGRU-ATT, HAN, LWAN, fail to predict relevant zero-shot labels (Table 2). This behavior is not surprising, because the training objective, minimizing binary cross-entropy across all labels, largely ignores infre-

quent labels. The zero-shot versions of CNN-LWAN and BIGRU-LWAN outperform all other methods on zero-shot labels, in line with the findings of Rios and Kavuluru (2018b), because they exploit label descriptors, which they do not update during training (Section 4.4). Exact Match also performs better than most other methods (excluding Z-CNN-LWAN and Z-BIGRU-LWAN) on zero-shot labels, because it exploits label descriptors.

To better support all types of labels (frequent, few-shot, zero-shot), we propose an ensemble of BIGRU-LWAN and Z-BIGRU-LWAN, which outputs the predictions of BIGRU-LWAN for frequent and few-shot labels, along with the predictions of Z-BIGRU-LWAN for zero-shot labels. The ensemble's results for 'all labels' in Table 2 are the same as those of BIGRU-LWAN, because zero-shot labels are very few (163) and rare in the test set.

The two methods (MAX-HSS, LW-HAN) that aggregate (via MAXPOOL) predictions across sections under-perform in all types of labels, suggesting that combining predictions from individual sections is not a promising direction for XMTC.

5.5 Providing Evidence through Attention

Chalkidis and Kampas (2018) noted that self-attention does not only lead to performance improvements in legal text classification, but might also provide useful evidence for the predictions (i.e., assisting in decision-making). On the left side of Figure 4a, we demonstrate such indicative results by visualizing the attention heat-maps of BIGRU-ATT and BIGRU-LWAN. Recall that BIGRU-LWAN uses a separate attention head per label. This allows producing multi-color heat-maps (a different color per label) separately indicating which words the system attends most when predicting each label. By contrast, BIGRU-ATT uses a single attention head and, thus, the result-

Figure 4: Attention heat-maps for BIGRU-ATT (left) and BIGRU-LWAN (right). Gold labels (concepts) are shown at the top of each sub-figure, while the top 5 predicted labels are shown at the bottom. Correct predictions are shown in bold. BIGRU-LWAN's label-wise attentions are depicted in different colors.

ing heat-maps include only one color.

6 Conclusions and Future Work

We compared various neural methods on a new legal XMTC dataset, EURLEX57K, also investigating few-shot and zero-shot learning. We showed that BIGRU-ATT is a strong baseline for this XMTC dataset, outperforming CNN-LWAN (Mullenbach et al., 2018), which was especially designed for XMTC, but that replacing the vanilla CNN of CNN-LWAN by a BIGRU encoder (BIGRU-LWAN) leads to the best overall results, except for zero-shot labels. For the latter, the zero-shot version of CNN-LWAN of Rios and Kavuluru (2018b) produces exceptional results, compared to the other methods, and its performance improves further when its CNN is replaced by a BIGRU (Z-BIGRU-LWAN). Surprisingly HAN (Yang et al., 2016) and other hierarchical methods we considered (MAX-HSS, LW-HAN) are weaker compared to the other neural methods we experimented with, which do not consider the structure (sections) of the documents.

The best methods of this work rely on GRUs and thus are computationally expensive. The length of the documents further affects the training time of these methods. Hence, we plan to investigate the use of Transformers (Vaswani et al., 2017; Dai et al., 2019) and dilated CNNs (Kalchbrenner et al., 2017) as alternative document encoders.

Given the recent advances in transfer learning for natural language processing, we plan to experiment with pre-trained neural language models for feature extraction and fine-tuning using state-of-the-art approaches such as ELMO (Peters et al., 2018)), ULMFIT (Howard and Ruder, 2018) and BERT (Devlin et al., 2019).

Finally, we also plan to investigate further the extent to which attention heat-maps provide useful explanations of the predictions made by legal predictive models following recent work on attention explainability (Jain and Wallace, 2019).

References

Nikolaos Aletras et al. 2016. Predicting judicial decisions of the European Court of Human Rights: a Natural Language Processing perspective. *PeerJ Computer Science*, 2:e93.

Kush Bhatia, Himanshu Jain, Purushottam Kar, Manik Varma, and Prateek Jain. 2015. Sparse Local Embeddings for Extreme Multi-label Classification. In *Advances in Neural Information Processing Systems 28*, pages 730–738.

Piotr Bojanowski, Edouard Grave, Armand Joulin, and Tomas Mikolov. 2016. Enriching Word Vectors with Subword Information. *arXiv preprint arXiv:1607.04606*.

Ilias Chalkidis, Ion Androutsopoulos, and Achilleas Michos. 2017. Extracting Contract Elements. In *Proceedings of the 16th International Conference on Artificial Intelligence and Law*, pages 19–28.

Ilias Chalkidis and Dimitrios Kampas. 2018. Deep learning in law: early adaptation and legal word embeddings trained on large corpora. *Artificial Intelligence and Law*.

Zihang Dai, Zhilin Yang, Yiming Yang, Jaime G. Carbonell, Quoc V. Le, and Ruslan Salakhutdinov. 2019. Transformer-XL: Attentive Language Models Beyond a Fixed-Length Context. *CoRR*, abs/1901.02860.

Jacob Devlin, Ming-Wei Chang, Kenton Lee, and Kristina Toutanova. 2019. BERT: Pre-training of Deep Bidirectional Transformers for Language Understanding. *Proceedings of the Conference of the NA Chapter of the Association for Computational Linguistics*.

Rotem Dror, Gili Baumer, Segev Shlomov, and Roi Reichart. 2018. The Hitchhiker's Guide to Testing Statistical Significance in Natural Language Processing. In *Proceedings of the 56th Annual Meeting of ACL (Long Papers)*, pages 1383–1392.

Jeremy Howard and Sebastian Ruder. 2018. Universal Language Model Fine-tuning for Text Classification. In *Proceedings of the 56th Annual Meeting of the Association for Computational Linguistics*, pages 328–339.

Sarthak Jain and Byron C. Wallace. 2019. Attention is not Explanation. *CoRR*, abs/1902.10186.

Alistair EW Johnson, David J. Stone, Leo A. Celi, and Tom J. Pollard. 2017. MIMIC-III, a freely accessible critical care database. *Nature*.

Nal Kalchbrenner, Lasse Espeholt, Karen Simonyan, Aäron van den Oord, Alex Graves, and Koray Kavukcuoglu. 2017. Neural Machine Translation in Linear Time. In *Proceedings of Conference on Empirical Methods in Natural Language Processing (EMNLP)*.

Yoon Kim. 2014. Convolutional Neural Networks for Sentence Classification. In *Proceedings of the 2014 Conference on Empirical Methods in Natural Language Processing (EMNLP)*, pages 1746–1751.

Diederik P. Kingma and Jim Ba. 2015. Adam: A method for stochastic optimization. In *Proceedings of the 5th International Conference on Learning Representations*.

David D. Lewis, Yiming Yang, Tony G. Rose, and Fan Li. 2004. RCV1: A New Benchmark Collection for Text Categorization Research. *Journal Machine Learning Research*, 5:361–397.

Jingzhou Liu, Wei-Cheng Chang, Yuexin Wu, and Yiming Yang. 2017. Deep Learning for Extreme Multi-label Text Classification. In *Proceedings of the 40th International ACM SIGIR Conference on Research and Development in Information Retrieval*, SIGIR '17, pages 115–124.

Yang Liu, Chengjie Sun, Lei Lin, and Xiaolong Wang. 2016. Learning Natural Language Inference using Bidirectional LSTM model and Inner-Attention. *arXiv preprint arXiv:1605.09090*, abs/1605.09090.

Christopher D. Manning, Prabhakar Raghavan, and Hinrich Schtze. 2009. *Introduction to Information Retrieval*. Cambridge University Press.

Julian McAuley and Jure Leskovec. 2013. Hidden Factors and Hidden Topics: Understanding Rating Dimensions with Review Text. In *Proceedings of the 7th ACM Conference on Recommender Systems*, RecSys '13, pages 165–172.

Eneldo Loza Mencia and Johannes Frnkranz. 2007. Efficient Multilabel Classification Algorithms for Large-Scale Problems in the Legal Domain. In *Proceedings of the LWA 2007*, pages 126–132.

James Mullenbach, Sarah Wiegreffe, Jon Duke, Jimeng Sun, and Jacob Eisenstein. 2018. Explainable Prediction of Medical Codes from Clinical Text. In *Proceedings of the 2018 Conference of the NA Chapter of the Association for Computational Linguistics: Human Language Technologies*, pages 1101–1111.

Ramesh Nallapati and Christopher D. Manning. 2008. Legal Docket Classification: Where Machine Learning Stumbles. In *EMNLP*, pages 438–446.

Ioannis Partalas, Aris Kosmopoulos, Nicolas Baskiotis, Thierry Artières, Georgios Paliouras, Éric Gaussier, Ion Androutsopoulos, Massih-Reza Amini, and Patrick Gallinari. 2015. LSHTC: A Benchmark for Large-Scale Text Classification. *CoRR*, abs/1503.08581.

Jeffrey Pennington, Richard Socher, and Christopher D. Manning. 2014. GloVe: Global Vectors for Word Representation. In *Empirical Methods in Natural Language Processing (EMNLP)*, pages 1532–1543.

Matthew E. Peters, Mark Neumann, Mohit Iyyer, Matt Gardner, Christopher Clark, Kenton Lee, and Luke Zettlemoyer. 2018. Deep contextualized word representations. In *Proceedings of the Conference of NA Chapter of the Association for Computational Linguistics*.

Yashoteja Prabhu and Manik Varma. 2014. FastXML: A Fast, Accurate and Stable Tree-classifier for Extreme Multi-label Learning. In *Proceedings of the 20th ACM SIGKDD International Conference on Knowledge Discovery and Data Mining*, KDD '14, pages 263–272.

Anthony Rios and Ramakanth Kavuluru. 2018a. EMR Coding with Semi-Parametric Multi-Head Matching Networks. In *Proceedings of the 2018 Conference of the NA Chapter of the Association for Computational Linguistics: Human Language Technologies*, pages 2081–2091.

Anthony Rios and Ramakanth Kavuluru. 2018b. Few-Shot and Zero-Shot Multi-Label Learning for Structured Label Spaces. In *Proceedings of the 2018 Conference on Empirical Methods in Natural Language Processing*, pages 3132–3142.

Tim Rocktäschel, Edward Grefenstette, Karl Moritz Hermann, Tomás Kociský, and Phil Blunsom. 2016. Reasoning about Entailment with Neural Attention. In *Proceedings of the 4th International Conference on Learning Representations (ICLR)*.

George Tsatsaronis, Georgios Balikas, Prodromos Malakasiotis, Ioannis Partalas, Matthias Zschunke, Michael R. Alvers, Dirk Weissenborn, Anastasia Krithara, Sergios Petridis, Dimitris Polychronopoulos, Yannis Almirantis, John Pavlopoulos, Nicolas Baskiotis, Patrick Gallinari, Thierry Artières, Axel-Cyrille Ngonga Ngomo, Norman Heino, Éric Gaussier, Liliana Barrio-Alvers, Michael Schroeder, Ion Androutsopoulos, and Georgios Paliouras. 2015. An overview of the BIOASQ large-scale biomedical semantic indexing and question answering competition. *BMC Bioinformatics*, 16(138).

Ashish Vaswani, Noam Shazeer, Niki Parmar, Jakob Uszkoreit, Llion Jones, Aidan N. Gomez, Lukasz Kaiser, and Illia Polosukhin. 2017. Attention Is All You Need. *Proceedings of the 31th Annual Conference on Neural Information Processing Systems*.

Kelvin Xu, Jimmy Ba, Ryan Kiros, Kyunghyun Cho, Aaron Courville, Ruslan Salakhudinov, Rich Zemel, and Yoshua Bengio. 2015. Show, Attend and Tell: Neural Image Caption Generation with Visual Attention. In *Proceedings of the 32nd International Conference on Machine Learning*, volume 37, pages 2048–2057.

Zichao Yang, Diyi Yang, Chris Dyer, Xiaodong He, Alex Smola, and Eduard Hovy. 2016. Hierarchical Attention Networks for Document Classification. In *Proceedings of the 2016 Conference of the NA Chapter of the Association for Computational Linguistics: Human Language Technologies*, pages 1480–1489.

Ronghui You, Suyang Dai, Zihan Zhang, Hiroshi Mamitsuka, and Shanfeng Zhu. 2018. AttentionXML: Extreme Multi-Label Text Classification with Multi-Label Attention Based Recurrent Neural Networks. *CoRR*, abs/1811.01727.

Peng Zhou, Wei Shi, Jun Tian, Zhenyu Qi, Bingchen Li, Hongwei Hao, and Bo Xu. 2016. Attention-Based Bidirectional Long Short-Term Memory Networks for Relation Classification. In *Proceedings of the 54th Annual Meeting of the Association for Computational Linguistics (Volume 2: Short Papers)*, pages 207–212.

Arkaitz Zubiaga. 2012. Enhancing Navigation on Wikipedia with Social Tags. *CoRR*, abs/1202.5469.

Author Index